Unfinished Learning

Unfinished Learning

Parents, Schools, and The COVID School Closures

Kristen J. Amundson

ROWMAN & LITTLEFIELD
Lanham • Boulder • New York • London

Published by Rowman & Littlefield
An imprint of The Rowman & Littlefield Publishing Group, Inc.
4501 Forbes Boulevard, Suite 200, Lanham, Maryland 20706
www.rowman.com

86-90 Paul Street, London EC2A 4NE, United Kingdom

British Library Cataloguing in Publication Information Available

Library of Congress Cataloging-in-Publication Data

Names: Amundson, Kristen J., author.
Title: Unfinished learning : parents, schools, and the covid school
    closures / Kristen J. Amundson.
Description: Lanham, Maryland : Rowman & Littlefield, 2022. | Includes
    index. | Summary: "Unfinished Learning explores what happened to
    families and to children during the pandemic school closures of 2020 and
    2021"—Provided by publisher.
Identifiers: LCCN 2022027343 (print) | LCCN 2022027344 (ebook) | ISBN
    9781475866728 (cloth) | ISBN 9781475866735 (paperback) | ISBN
    9781475866742 (epub)
Subjects: LCSH: School and home—United States. | Social distancing (Public
    health) and education—United States. | COVID-19 Pandemic, 2020—United
    States.
Classification: LCC LC225.3 .A68 2022 (print) | LCC LC225.3 (ebook) | DDC
    371.19/20973—dc23/eng/20220718
LC record available at https://lccn.loc.gov/2022027343
LC ebook record available at https://lccn.loc.gov/2022027344

Contents

Dedicated to my daughter Sara—
Everything I know about parenting,
I probably learned at your expense

ACKNOWLEDGMENTS

Writing *Unfinished Learning* has given me a new appreciation for how hard a job it is to be a parent, and how particularly hard it was during the pandemic. On top of all the usual parental challenges, the COVID parents also had to refresh their memories on long division and figure out how to manage multiple passwords and logins, all while trying to do their own work.

In writing this book, I called people—many of them complete strangers— and asked them if they were willing to talk openly and honestly about what turned out to have been one of the hardest years of their life. Astonishingly, many of them said yes.

They shared stories that were touching. Some of them broke my heart. But they also retain a great faith in their children's ability to overcome what they had to deal with. And because I've had a chance to hear their stories, I'm pretty confident they will.

Thank you to all the parents and grandparents I spoke to in writing this book: Mary Robb Wilson, Kwame B., Elena Guarinello, Sarah Johnson, Carole Uecker, Jennifer and Matt McNerney, Spencer Potter, Rebecca Geller, Nicole Christensen, Kara Stup, Myralyn McCabe, Lisa Juliar, Suzann Gallagher, Aimee Drewry, Margaret Millar, and Lindsay Dworkin, as well as that wonderful mom from Wells Fargo Bank who gave me the confidence that I was on the right track.

Thanks to Leia Surovell for an in-the-classroom take on how a tech failure affected students. Thanks to Dan Domenech for national insights into how schools coped, and to Reg Leichty for wisdom on All Things Tech. Shelley Reynolds and Myralyn McCabe gave me insights into how teachers coped. Carol Basile, dean and professor at the Mary Lou Fulton Teachers College at Arizona State University (MLFTC) helped me think about new ways schools might be organized.

Vladimir Kogan, assistant professor at Ohio State University, drew the line between local news organizations and informed voters in school board elections. My friend and former legislative seat mate Bob Brink was the source of much of my insight into where Virginia voted in 2021.

Astrid Garcia provided a sympathetic view of how immigrant parents coped. My friends at EduTutorVA continue to inspire me in thinking about how we can help kids catch up from the COVID closures.

Thanks to Tom Koerner and everyone at Rowman & Littlefield. They are great partners.

Finally and always, thanks to my daughter, Sara. She remains a thought partner and the occasional truth teller ("Just get back to writing, Mom").

INTRODUCTION

What did you do during the Revolution?
I survived.

—Emmanuel-Joseph Sieyes

This book is about what happened to families and to children during the pandemic school closures of 2020 and 2021. It's about the aftermath of children spending all that time out of school. And it's about the changing nature of the parent-school relationship.

I started writing *Unfinished Learning* with a simple premise: the pandemic was hard for everyone, but much harder for families with kids. Someone needed to tell their story.

But as the writing slogged on, I wondered if anyone would be interested in reading stories about COVID and school closures. Kids were back in school buildings, stores and businesses were opening up. Was the pandemic simply old news?

Then a phone call with someone I didn't know helped me see that for many families, COVID was not really over. It was March of 2022, and I was on the phone with my bank trying to track down one of those forms that accountants always seem to need and I can never find. I'd never spoken to the banker before, but she was friendly and as she was waiting for information to load onto her computer, we started chatting about how we were both recovering from two years of COVID.

"I'm not over it yet," she said. "I had my second grader at home for a year. It was so hard for him and for me. And I'm not sure he's back to where he should be in school."

That is the story I heard from parents all over the country. Even for the parents who had the good fortune to be able to work at home, trying to combine parenting with long division with Zoom meetings for work was exhausting.

After kids got back in school, the parents still worried about whether they had been able to do enough to help their kids learn.

In my research, I talked with families from across the country. Their children ranged from preschool to high school. I spoke with teachers and school administrators and policy experts. In the section on the Virginia election, I also talked with some Virginia political experts.

Most of the families, by their own admission, began the pandemic in a position of privilege. They had computers and internet access. At least one parent in each family had a job that allowed them to work from home.

And yet these families still struggled. The demands of combining their own work with helping one or more children with their schoolwork became more and more challenging as the weeks of school closure stretched on.

Families of children with disabilities had their own struggles. I could probably have written an entire book on how students with disabilities were affected by pandemic school closures. Often the educational supports these students need while they are in class were unavailable. In-person instructional assistants, physical therapists, and other support team members simply couldn't work as well—or sometimes at all—in a virtual environment.

One of the repeating themes of the stories about students with disabilities is the massive commitment their families made to help them during the pandemic. They quit jobs. They paid thousands of dollars in private tutors. They simply did not give up on their kids, even when they sometimes felt that the schools might be. Of the long-lasting educational consequences of COVID, the decline in academic performance by students with disabilities is likely to be one of the hardest to remedy.

It was clear that parents who did not have the privilege of working from home faced many more challenges. While they turned out to be reluctant to share their experiences for a book, I did interview teachers and staff members at nonprofit organizations to understand how they were affected. It's important to let their voices be heard in this book because their experiences were so much more daunting.

Unfinished Learning is also about the political fallout of school closures. There were two major elections in the immediate aftermath of school closures. Parents played a major role in both of them. Political pundits, who did figure out that parents were *really mad* about something nonetheless seem to have missed what it is parents were mad about.

Mark Twain once said, "If a cat sits on a hot stove, that cat won't sit on a hot stove again. That cat won't sit on a cold stove either." The cat learned a lesson by sitting on the stove, but it was the wrong lesson. My sense is that both political parties, in their desire to win (or win back) the parent vote, may also be learning the wrong lesson. With the help of some polling data and some post-election focus groups, as well as my talks with parents across the country, I'm trying to put those elections into some perspective as well.

A few notes about writing style. First, I made a conscious decision not to use children's names in this book. Certainly, parents are legally authorized to give consent to use their child's name, and of course I always ask if I can have permission even to tell their story. But I began worrying about the kid who gets to middle school and suddenly is confronted with a Google search from the class Mean Girl revealing that they struggled in math in the second grade. I figured I'd just spare everyone that particular trauma.

Second, I stuck with a decision I made in an earlier book to use the singular "they." I cited no less an authority than Benjamin Dreyer, copy chief at Random House, in his wonderful style manual *Dreyer's English.* (Buy it if you don't own it.) "The singular 'they,'" he writes, "is not the wave of the future; it's the wave of the present."[1]

And to reinforce that statement, you'll notice that several of the people I interview in this book prefer the pronouns "they/their." So if you're not used to using "they" as a singular pronoun, you'll be a little more used to it after reading this book.

Finally, I adopted a practice that Jay Mathews, the wonderful education writer for the *Washington Post*, has always generously used with interview subjects: I showed them what I was going to include in the book before it went to the publisher. They were both helpful and amazingly light-handed in their suggestions for changes. They corrected a few flat-out factual errors, noting that a kid was in third grade, not second, or a student was enrolled in School District A rather than School District B. In one case, a mom pointed out a sentence that was really remarkably clunky and confusing upon a second reading. (It came out of the manuscript.) But other than that, the families provided only the confirmation that I was telling their story in as truthful a way as I could.

Unfinished Learning was completed almost exactly two years from the day schools first closed. While some things are back to normal, with students in class and parents back in the office, there are still many lingering effects of the pandemic. More than two hundred thirty thousand children have lost parents or secondary caregivers to COVID.[2] The number is likely higher, according to Dan Treglia, a social-science researcher at the University of Pennsylvania. "This is a problem in every state and every community, yet some groups have been hit harder. Black and Hispanic children lose caregivers at rates more than double those of white children."[3]

Students are now arriving in school with a host of social and emotional problems. "Teachers are seeing behaviors they have never seen before," said Carol Basile, dean and director of Arizona State University's Mary Lou Fulton Teachers College. In October of 2021, the American Academy of

Pediatrics, the American Academy of Child and Adolescent Psychiatry, and the Children's Hospital Association declared that the pandemic-related decline in child and adolescent mental health has become a national emergency.[4]

Academically, reports on students' learning loss continued to get worse during the 2021–2022 school year. A national survey of teachers conducted in December 2021 found that seven in ten were less confident than before the pandemic that they would be able to help their students reach grade level by the end of the year.[5]

But the biggest and longest-lasting impact of the COVID school closures may be a fraying of the relationship between schools and parents. Across the country, parents are showing up in schools and at school board meetings to protest everything from book selection to mask mandates to admission to specialized schools. The Education Week Research Center reported that more than 40 percent of school administrators said that principals or the superintendent in their district had been physically or verbally threatened over their COVID responses.[6]

Statistics like those make the book feel a bit like what lawyers call a "parade of horribles"—an unending litany of bad things. The truth of the matter is that a lot of COVID felt like a parade of horribles. But there are some lessons to be learned, and I end the book with those.

Mostly, this is a book about some parents who were honest and open and trusting enough to share their stories with me. I have worked hard to tell those stories with the sensitivity and the honesty they deserve.

I started writing *Unfinished Learning* with a sense of admiration for parents and how they helped their kids through the pandemic. I end it with something more like awe.

CHAPTER 1

MARCH 13, 2020

The jittery focus, the devastated shelves, a couple of fights breaking out
over paper towels . . . madness in people's eyes—it was like the beginning
of every show where the streets empty and some grotesque magic entity
emerges from mist or fire.

—Louise Erdrich, *The Sentence*

On March 13, 2020, Mary Robb Wilson was working her normal volunteer
shift in her daughter's kindergarten classroom in St. Helena, California.
Midway through the morning, the teacher asked her to start assembling
folders of worksheets the children could take home. There was a rumor that
schools might be closed for a little while.

In Fairfax, Virginia, Jennifer and Matt McNerney's two children were
surprised by an unexpected extra day of spring break. The schools were
scheduled to go on break starting the following Monday, but a tweet sent
out from the school account at 11:34 p.m. on Thursday, March 12, read: "All
FCPS schools will be closed Friday, March 13, 2020. School offices and central offices will open on time with an unscheduled leave policy in effect for
12-month employees. More details to follow." There were no further classes
for a full month.

In San Francisco, Spencer Potter and his wife, Krista Walton Potter, were
both in their offices when Krista texted the news that schools would be closing
for "*three whole weeks*," Potter said. They informed their offices that they'd
be working remotely for that time, feeling grateful to have that option. And
then they went online and ordered some home schooling supplies. They had
grand ambitions for how they could do school activities at home. For a while.

In suburban Richmond, Virginia, Kwame B. and his wife knew they were
going to have to help their rising kindergartener readjust his expectations
about starting school in Chesterfield County the next year. It was something
he'd been looking forward to and talking about for a long time. "For him, the

whole concept of going to school entailed getting on a big yellow school bus, going to a school building, and having time to play with friends." Although the parents both hoped that school would be back in session by the time kindergarten started in the fall, they decided it might be a good idea to help their son envision a different reality, just in case. (That proved prescient. In Chesterfield, the schools did not fully resume in-person learning until mid-April of 2021.)

When the Montgomery County, Maryland, schools announced they were closing, Elena Guarinello and Jessica Latterman figured that it was going to be a short disruption to their family schedule. Their second grader was fairly adept on the computer, and the two of them were able to work from home. They had plenty of books and activities to occupy their daughter's non-school time. They weren't worried. After all, how long could schools stay closed?

With three kids in elementary school and two demanding jobs, Rebecca Geller and Brad Cheney approached the shift to virtual learning the same way they tackled everything else: they made lists. They knew there would be some lag time before the Fairfax County schools started up in virtual mode. They didn't know at the time that they would have an entire month to fill, but they prepared for a longer-than-normal spring break. "We tried to do one substantive learning activity every day," Rebecca said. "We did science experiments. We watched the Mo Willems classes sponsored by the Kennedy Center. We found a virtual yoga class. Like every other family in the country, we made sourdough starter—but, hey, it was also kind of a science project, right?" They made a quarantine bucket list of all the things they were hoping to do. Some were chores to accomplish, like cleaning out old toys. Others were fun, like scheduling a regular family reading time. They tried to get outside. Their main goal was to keep their kids involved with learning in the real world. "Who wants a kid to be sitting in front of a screen for ten hours a day?"

Because Nicole Christensen owned a fitness business in Boulder, Colorado, she already had an inkling that the COVID numbers in the state were heading in the wrong direction for schools to stay open. On the day when the Boulder Valley School District announced it was moving to virtual learning, she and her husband Eric made a decision. "We had zero interest in putting our kindergartener in front of a computer screen," she said. "We don't let our kids watch TV and they don't have an iPad. Why would we want to do school that way?"

In the first week of March 2020, Kara Stup had an IEP meeting with the team at her son's Richmond, Virginia, school. He was in sixth grade, the first year of middle school, and his adjustment had been uneven. "The teacher's style and the classroom atmosphere are important for my son, who has autism. When things are calm and organized, he just does better."

The transition from an elementary school with one teacher of record to a middle school with many teachers had been a challenge. "But we talked about some adjustments we thought we could make before the end of the year. That would help him get off to a stronger start in seventh grade," she said.

They never had a chance to find out if the adjustments would have worked. Schools shut down a week later. Her son would not be in a classroom again for more than a year.

Myralyn McCabe is a self-described "teacher mom" in Flagstaff, Arizona. When her school district announced they would be closing for COVID, she went into her classroom to "grab whatever I could so I could teach for what I thought would be a few weeks." She and her students were in the middle of a clay project, so her classroom was filled with little unfired clay creations. She wondered how she should get them in the kiln so her students could take them home. Her second-grade son would be learning at home while she was trying to teach. Even though he was fairly tech savvy, she wondered if he'd have enough to do.

When schools closed in the spring of 2020 as part of the nationwide response to the coronavirus, almost no one envisioned that for fifty million students, the "temporary" school closures would turn out to be anything but. By early May, forty-eight states (all but Montana and Wyoming), four US territories, the District of Columbia, and the Department of Defense Education Activity ordered or recommended school building closures for the rest of their academic year.

Here's how it happened:

In January, there were rumors of a new virus spreading rapidly through China. On January 29, *Education Week*, often viewed as the newspaper of record for K–12 education, carried its first story about a few schools and districts that were beginning to take precautions to limit students' exposure to the virus.[1] The story noted that some school districts were beginning to send parents information on how to prevent the spread of the virus, including hand washing and "staying away from sick people."

In mid-February, a few schools, largely concentrated in Washington and New York, closed temporarily. These short closures allowed school custodial staff to conduct deep cleaning in school buildings.

On February 25, Nancy Messonnier, director of the National Center for Immunization and Respiratory Diseases at the CDC, held a press briefing on the impending threat from the coronavirus. "It's not a question of if this will happen but when this will happen and how many people in this country will have severe illnesses," she said. "Disruptions to everyday life may be severe, but people might want to start thinking about that now. You should ask your children's school about their plans for school dismissals or school closures.

Ask if there are plans for teleschool. I contacted my local school superintendent this morning with exactly those questions."[2]

On March 3, Dr. Anne Schuchat, the principal deputy director of the CDC, and Dr. Anthony Fauci addressed a hearing of the Senate Health, Education, Labor, and Pensions (HELP) Committee. Dr. Schuchat described the guidance that the CDC was giving to schools:

> The general principle is to minimize disruption. You have this balance between the earlier you act the more impact it can have in slowing the spread and the enormous disruption we see with school closures. You may remember in 2009, we saw hundreds of thousands of students sent home in the first couple weeks of the pandemic. As we learned more about the virus . . . we realized that was too disruptive. . . . We've dialed that back to instead shift to staying home when you're sick . . . trying to keep classes going because so many depend on school lunches and other services that are at school.[3]

These were early warnings that the virus might affect schools. On March 3, 2020, *Education Week* ran an article that in retrospect seems prescient: "Coronavirus Prompting E-Learning Strategies."[4] The story outlined lessons learned by schools in China and Hong Kong.

It also laid out some advice for schools as they considered a move to virtual schooling and told the story of the Rensselaer Central Schools in Indiana. A severe flu outbreak had forced schools to close for two days. Superintendent Curtis Craig advised other school leaders, "If you can run the kids through some online practice while they're here at school, it's much, much better. If online isn't completely different than what they're doing in school, that's even better," Craig said. "If the kids are used to going to a student-management system to go online to submit their assignments, then it's not a completely different experience for them."

In hindsight, it's clear that schools had less than two weeks to implement Craig's recommendations. The virus continued to spread rapidly throughout the United States. By March 11—just eight days after Dr. Schuchat recommended a balanced approach to considering school closures—the World Health Organization declared that COVID-19 was a pandemic. The next day, Ohio governor Mike DeWine closed the state's schools.

"Everything," said Kwame B., about the schools in his suburban community, "just came to a screeching halt." No one knew when schools would reopen. (The notion that they would be closed until the end of the school year seemed remote; the thought that many schools would not open their doors again for a year was almost unimaginable.) And yet, by March 25, all the schools in the United States were closed, and by mid-April, nearly all states announced that they would remain closed through the end of the school year.

With almost no warning, schools had to transition from the traditional teacher-in-the-classroom model of learning to the kids-at-home-on-the-couch model. Results were . . . uneven. These closures, made quickly and with little time for parents to prepare for the change, ultimately affected more than fifty-five million students in one hundred twenty-four thousand public and private schools throughout the United States.[5]

School closures did not occur in a vacuum. The issues that were to plague virtual learning were all in place on March 11, the day before Ohio's governor issued the first statewide order to close schools. Some students and schools entered pandemic school closures already at a disadvantage. Students were not performing on grade level. Their schools were under-resourced. They had limited access to technology. And school closures brought all these issues to the fore and made them worse.

TECHNOLOGY ACCESS

Initially, most school districts thought the closures would last for only a few weeks. So extending spring break or sending home paper packets of learning activities initially seemed like a way to manage.

But then the closures dragged on, and schools began to realize the magnitude of the challenge they would face in getting students learning again. Schools moved online in March. But for millions of students, that was the day that the door effectively closed on learning.

Reaching and then teaching students proved to be hard nearly everywhere. And it was much harder for the students who most needed consistent teaching: students who were already below grade level, English learners, and students living in poverty. Those were, sadly, the students least likely to have access to the technology they would need to stay connected to their schools.

Roughly 3.1 million households with children had no broadband connection at home that would be sufficient to allow online learning. Broadband adoption rates in Black and Latino or Hispanic households lagged behind white households.

In New York City, at the start of the pandemic three hundred thousand students lived in homes with no computer. In Philadelphia, so many students lacked access to technology that the superintendent initially decided that there would be no online classes because they would only widen the inequity. (The district later announced that instead, it would distribute devices to children who lacked them.) That decision, of course, did nothing about the fact that devices would not work without a connection to high-speed internet.

In other words, said the Brookings Institution in a March 2020 report, "As COVID-19 [required] more schools to transition to online learning, the students who were already the most vulnerable to falling behind [would] face even more hurdles to keep pace."[6]

Many of Myralyn McCabe's students lived outside of Flagstaff. "On the Navajo reservation where some of our students lived," she says, "the internet was spotty. Our school did not yet have internet hotspots for the kids. When kids wanted to check in with the school, they'd have to drive to a little town called Loop. Then they'd sit in the parking lot of the school because it was the only internet connection they had available."

Even teachers lacked the technology that would allow them to teach online. That was particularly true in schools serving low-income students and students of color. A RAND survey of K–12 public school teachers and principals found that nearly twice as many principals in high-poverty schools reported a "major" or "very major" need for technology for students *and for teachers* compared with those in low-poverty schools. Many of the differences in the quality of supports schools could provide stemmed from "preexisting differences in access to such resources as high-speed internet and computing devices (e.g., laptops or tablets)."[7] Chapter 3 describes how schools tackled the technology problems.

LEARNING GAPS—"WE HAVEN'T SEEN FINE, EVER."

There was a general, if often unspoken, understanding about the inequities in education before the pandemic caused schools to close. "COVID just revealed how serious those inequities are," said Bridget Terry Long, the Saris Professor of Education and Economics and Dean of the Harvard Graduate School of Education. "School closures disproportionately hurt low-income students, students with special needs, and school systems that are under-resourced."[8]

The pandemic laid bare one of the biggest structural issues in funding education: because property taxes are a major source of funding for most schools, there are simply fewer dollars available to support students in low-income districts. One 2019 study by EdBuild, a nonprofit organization that focused on education funding, found that predominantly white districts got $23 billion more than their nonwhite counterparts serving about the same number of students.[9] That meant more money for teacher salaries, for school buildings, and for computers.

The problem of resource inequity was magnified because of the additional responsibilities that schools have taken on. "You think about schools and academics, but what COVID really made clear was that schools do so much more than that," said Long. A child's school, she stressed "is social, emotional support. It's safety. It's the food system. It is health care."

Anna Baros, a middle school teacher in Tulsa, Oklahoma, was clear-eyed about what her school and students faced in March of 2020. "We haven't seen fine, ever," she said. Long before the pandemic, students at her school, particularly students of color and those with disabilities, were "already so underserved."[10]

Not all schools offered students the same learning opportunities. Particularly in schools that served low-income students and students of color, teachers were likely to be less experienced. There were fewer computers. Their schools offered fewer rigorous courses, and if these courses were available, they were often discouraged from enrolling. Black students, for example, accounted for 14.2 percent of high school seniors in 2020. But they made up just 8.3 percent of the students who sat for an Advanced Placement (AP) exam.[11]

The U.S. Department of Education's review of the impact of COVID school closures highlighted other long-standing disparities. In 2015–2016, for example, while half of all high schools offered a course in calculus and 60 percent offered a course in physics, those figures dropped to 38 percent and 51 percent respectively in schools serving a large number of Black and Latino students. Unsurprisingly, then, Black students accounted for just 8 percent of students enrolled in calculus although they made up 16 percent of total high school enrollment.

In earlier grades, disparities also were evident. While Black students accounted for 17 percent of all eighth graders, they were only 11 percent of the students enrolled in eighth grade algebra, and just 9 percent of the students who successfully completed the course.[12]

Students did not start at the same place when schools shut down. The average Black or Latino student was roughly two years behind the average white student, and low-income students continued to lag behind students from more affluent families prior to the pandemic. One study concluded, "Achievement gaps between the top and bottom quartiles of the SES distribution have been large and remarkably constant for a near half century."[13]

One of the lessons of school closures was that they had a disparate impact on both families and children. Parents who could work only when their children were in school were left in the lurch. As Washington Senator Patty Murray said in the HELP Committee hearings,

As is so often the case, this public threat will have hidden and higher costs for those who are low wage workers, who don't have affordable childcare, who don't have health insurance, and who are experiencing homelessness. In my home state, people are being told to stay home for two weeks if they are sick. There are not tests, so they can't get tested. Guess who can't stay home? If you don't have childcare, if you're a low wage worker, if you don't have sick leave. When those people's basic needs are not met, they cannot make choices to protect themselves, which means they can't make choices that best protect others too, because one person getting sick has repercussions for all of those around them.[14]

Chapter 5 discusses the long-lasting impact of school closures on the students who started out behind. By the end of the pandemic, the existing achievement gaps had widened.

BIGGEST CHALLENGES FOR STUDENTS WITH DISABILITIES

For the roughly 14 percent of public school students who need additional support to learn, pandemic closures were even more difficult. Many students with Individualized Education Plans (IEPs) require hands-on instructional support. They need physical or cognitive therapy. For school districts that struggled just to get students logged on to their system, adapting the wide range of special education services to online learning platforms was simply a bridge too far, at least during the early months.

After years of advocating on behalf of her son, Lisa Juliar was finally pleased with his educational placement. Her son, then a high school junior, was born with a rare chromosomal disorder called Cri du Chat that affected his speech and language and left him unable to speak. Doctors had originally told the family that their son might never walk, talk, or learn. But technology, in the form of an iPad app, had allowed him to communicate and learn. Finally, Mounds View School District in suburban St. Paul had placed him in fully integrated classrooms. He was taking academic classes, learning the bones in the body and the geography of the continents. He was thriving.

His Individualized Education Plan (IEP) included specific learning goals in classes like science and history. That was a change from an early IEP that had included only two learning goals: first, that he learn to skip in three different ways; and second, that he learn to clean the lunch room tables by himself.

"He had done an interview with a large biomedical firm and had an upcoming interview for a job at a car dealership that was part of his special education preparation for work," Juliar said. "We were finally in a good place."

In Fairfax County, Suzann Gallagher and her husband, Richard, had worked hard to get their son the support he needed. "Our fourth-grade son has both ADHD and dyslexia. We had worked with the school to get the right support system for him. In addition, we hired a private tutor to work one-on-one, focusing on literacy. All of that was coming together and he was starting to make progress, particularly in reading."

Then schools closed. "When school stopped, all that support stopped. And his progress just came crashing down."

Most of the social services for children are, one way or another, connected to the schools. School meals feed millions of children breakfast and lunch. Dental care, mental health care, and therapy services of all types: physical therapy, occupational, and speech therapy are all provided largely through special education programs. School counselors make referrals for families who need connection to welfare agencies or housing for homeless families.

But as Gallagher points out, school closures meant that all those additional services also closed up shop. In addition to learning loss, families were facing a loss of many other basic services they needed to survive. That meant food-insecure children could no longer rely on school breakfast and lunch. Children who lacked access to health care could not visit the school nurse. Students who received school-based mental health services were also cut off.

In addition to figuring out how to keep students learning academic content, communities rallied to address those other challenges. Chapter 2 describes how the school lunch program made a successful shift from a place-based, rule-bound program to a much more nimble and family-centric program delivering food to food-insecure children. Meeting other nonacademic needs, however, was often much more difficult.

HOW EUROPEAN SCHOOLS COPED WITH COVID

At the time schools closed in March, there was general agreement that taking this action was one important way to reduce infection rates and flatten the curve of new infections. But prolonged school closures are "one of the most disruptive forces in the COVID-19 era," noted researchers in the journal *World Medical & Health Policy.* And as time went on, school closures "upended life for children and families, and they left educators forced to determine quickly how to remotely educate students in an equitable manner."[15]

From the earliest days of the pandemic, European countries worked hard to keep schools open as a priority. "The school environment, in our perception, is still quite a controlled environment," he said. "We think it's better to have schools open than to send kids home, have them meet on the street and give them more opportunities to spread the virus," Steven Van Gucht, the head of viral diseases at Belgium's national public health institute, told the *Washington Post* in September of 2020.[16]

Typically, European countries attacked the spread of the virus as a problem for the entire society rather than just for the schools. Many countries implemented nationwide lockdowns to control the spread of COVID. In Europe, those countries included France, Germany, the United Kingdom, Italy, Spain,

Belgium, Switzerland, and many Eastern European countries. Scandinavian countries were more likely to institute localized closures.

School closures were seen as *part* of the nationwide effort to control transmission of the virus. In Europe, reopening schools was almost always the top priority (or one of the top priorities) when things began to ease.

European schools used a wide variety of approaches to bring students back to school. These varied from limiting the grades involved in reopening (younger students only, older students only, or all students). They varied schedules by alternating shifts or staggering opening and closing times. They also implemented a number of transmission control measures including mandating face masks, encouraging hand washing, and creating physical distance.

In Norway, for example, schools were closed on March 11, 2020. Reopening of schools started on April 20 for kindergarten students followed on April 27 by students in grades one through four. The government recommended that classes be limited to no more than fifteen students. Special precautions include having children wash their desks daily. Some schools divided their playgrounds.[17]

"The view in Norway is that children and youth should have high priority to have as normal a life as possible, because this disease is going to last," she said. "They have the lowest burden of the disease, so they shouldn't have the highest burden of measures," Margrethe Greve-Isdahl, a senior physician at the Norwegian Institute of Public Health, who was responsible for Norway's guidelines to prevent infections in schools, told the *Washington Post*.[18] Even after schools reopened for younger students, there was no significant increase in the growth rate of COVID cases.

European nations also collected and used data to limit transmission. When school closures were part of an overall community effort, they seem to have had that effect. Reopening of schools for all students in countries with low community transmission (Denmark and Norway) has not resulted in a significant increase in the growth rate of COVID-19 cases.[19]

From the beginning, the United States was different.

In the first three months of 2020, few Americans knew much about the COVID-19 virus. Health agencies had to convey important information about what was known and how people could protect themselves and their loved ones from getting sick. This communications challenge was made more difficult by the constantly changing nature of what scientists were learning about the virus.

There was by early April a concerted federal effort to transfer responsibility (and blame) for the growing COVID death count to the states. In an April 2 letter to Senator Charles Schumer of New York, the president wrote, "As you are aware, the Federal Government is merely a back-up for state governments."[20]

Instead of a coordinated federal strategy, decisions about everything from reopening schools to purchasing personal protective equipment were to be left to states. It became clear that the priority in many states seemed to be reopening businesses as soon as possible. As epidemiologist Jennifer Nuzzo and pediatrician Joshua Sharfstein said in a *New York Times* opinion piece, "The way states lifted social distancing restrictions imposed to fight the coronavirus sadly demonstrates our priorities. Officials let bars, restaurants, and gyms open, despite warnings from public health experts that these environments pose the greatest risk for spreading the disease."[21]

A VERY, VERY EXTENDED SPRING BREAK

When families left their schools in mid-March, they had no idea it would be nearly a year before most of them returned. During that time, they would struggle to help their children learn how to master (OK, adjust to) (OK, survive) online learning. They helped a kindergartener (who hadn't learned to read) figure out how to log on to a class website. They set up learning pods. They started Facebook groups. They got politically active.

And they waited (and waited) for schools to reopen so they could take their kids back to the classrooms they left. Some of them never would, opting instead to enroll their children in a different school or to create small learning pods instead. One family even moved halfway across the country to find a school that better suited their children.

But mostly, they coped. And they adjusted their expectations for what the next few weeks were likely to look like.

The day that Fairfax County announced they would close schools a day early, Aimee Drewry and her husband, Seth, made the decision that they would start their spring break a little early. So they packed up the car, made sure everyone had KN95 masks, and started driving south to Orlando, where her parents lived. "Our plan was that my mom, a retired kindergarten teacher, would help with the kids while we got some work done. We felt better just knowing there was a plan," Aimee recalled.

Sarah Johnson had received an email from the Bedford, Massachusetts, school district's superintendent on March 12 stating that "out of an abundance of caution," the schools in the district would be closed for two weeks starting March 13. She reached out to her office's HR department, noting that she would need to work remotely for the duration of the school closure, which the district estimated would be roughly two weeks. On the first day of the school closure, since there was no guidance about social distancing or masking, she and her two oldest daughters went swimming in the community indoor pool.

For Margaret and Tom Millar, school closures came near the end of a kindergarten year that was rocky for their son even before the pandemic. He is an active child who sometimes had trouble sitting still for long periods, and in parent-teacher conferences, his teacher seemed not to know him very well. As the year progressed, it became clear he just didn't want to go to school most days. When Fairfax County tacked an extra day onto their regularly scheduled spring break, the Millars weren't worried. If anything, it came as something of a relief.

In a St. Louis suburb, the Reliford family looked forward to the weekend with great anticipation. It was finally their turn to host the class pets, two mice named Snowball and Chubbs. Because the weekend was the start of spring break, they were happy to get the mice for an extra week.

But spring break never really ended. "We were just going to take them for spring break, but we took them forever, apparently," said Stacy Reliford. By mid-summer, her hope was that the mice could go to middle school in the fall. She also hoped her children would go with them.[22]

CHAPTER 2

THE COVID SPRING

Remember: We're all in this alone.

—Lily Tomlin

School closures were meant to be temporary. Schools gave parents very little warning of an extended closure because school leaders honestly believed students would be out of the classroom for only a week or two.

Sarah Johnson said that when she received an email from the school superintendent in Bedford, Massachusetts, saying that, as in several neighboring districts, the schools would temporarily close, "I really, truly, in my head thought that not every district in Massachusetts would close and that it would be about two weeks," she said.

But although parents and school administrators didn't know it, the school year had effectively ended for fifty million US students. As it became clear that schools would not reopen any time soon, districts struggled to provide an alternative.

Initially, many teachers sent home some sort of file folder filled with learning activities. But teachers were unable to come into the school because the buildings were closed. That left districts scrambling to find a digital alternative.

It was a huge problem. Some students needed devices. Some lacked internet connectivity. Teachers had little or no time to transform lessons that might work well in a classroom setting to a virtual setting. And parents just needed to figure out how they could get their kids online.

There are many lessons to learn from the rollout of virtual learning across the country. But they can probably be summed up this way: for "online learning" to work, students need to be (a) online and (b) learning.

For many students, neither was true. Even before COVID, students needed computers and connectivity to do their basic schoolwork. Many stayed after school to use computers and the internet for their homework. Well before the pandemic, in 2018, research showed that 70 percent of American teachers assigned homework that required access to the internet, and half of all students said they needed such access every day.[1]

Schools had been working for years to achieve a 1:1 ratio of students to computers. But school budgets were always stretched, and school technology staff was always small and overworked. Ensuring that students had access to computers and tablets was a slow and expensive process.

School closures made the abstract conversations about the "digital divide" starkly real. However well-intentioned they were, many schools simply did not have enough computers to get them to every student. A survey conducted by the EdWeek Research Center found that in roughly one-third of districts, there were not enough school devices to make one available to every middle and high school student. One in ten districts reported that they had only one device for every four students.[2]

In elementary schools, the ratio was even worse. Fewer than half (42 percent) of educators said they worked in a school that owned enough tablets and devices for every student.[3]

Throughout the spring and summer of 2020, schools made what can only be described as heroic efforts to get devices into the hands of children. But they ran into supply-chain issues that lingered into the fall of the following school year. The chips that made everything from iPads to cars work were in short supply. At one point, there were simply no Chrome books (the low-cost tablet that is a favorite of schools) to be purchased anywhere.

Even when devices and tablets were in students' hands, not all of them could get online. They also needed a way to *connect* that device to the internet. Students without home internet access, including those who relied only on a mobile plan to be online, spent more time on their homework, had lower grade point averages, and had weaker digital skills, even after controlling for socioeconomic factors that potentially influence academic performance, according to a Michigan State University study. They were also less likely to plan to attend a college or university.[4]

However, high-speed internet connections are expensive, and many families could not afford them. Even though there were some programs to provide online access to low-income families, they were not always publicized. And then there were the broad swaths of the country where high-speed internet connections were simply unavailable.

Shortly before the COVID school closures in 2019, 15 percent of US households with school-age children lacked high-speed internet at home. The problem was particularly acute for low-income families: One in three households earning below $30,000 a year lacked internet.[5]

So families made do. In Saginaw, Michigan, for example, the owner of a fast-food restaurant said he could always tell when his local schools were nearing the end of a marking period and about to start exams. That was when students without access to the internet would come into his restaurant, bringing their laptops, their tablets, or in some cases their smart phones. Students who could afford to purchase food sat in the booth making their soft drinks or their fries last as long as possible, all while they took advantage of the restaurant's free Wi-Fi. Families who could not afford to buy anything to eat sat in the parking lot, trying to catch a signal to help their children complete basic school assignments.[6]

There were other students who had to rely on a smart phone. They were most likely to come from a low-income family or a family where parents had a high school education or less, according to the National Center for Education Statistics.[7] When I talked with teens who have done homework this way, they all agreed that it is simply impossible to answer an AP history data base question on a cell phone.

In rural areas, where there was often even less access to high-speed internet, students struggled to get online when school went virtual. In Minnesota, the Duluth schools worked hard to provide Chrome Books to students who did not own their own device. "There were a lot of students who needed computers," said Carol Uecker, a grandmother of a student who was in the eighth grade when the pandemic hit. Even when students could get a computer, and supply-chain issues meant that for some students there would be no device until fall, the school district had no way to make sure those students could access the high-speed internet needed to do online school.

The district opened the high school auditorium and created learning stations at least six feet apart so students could do virtual learning from the school building. Other families sat outside local libraries. "They were trying to do school in their car," Uecker said. Still others sat outside the local McDonald's to take advantage of their Wi-Fi.

Even in affluent Fairfax County, library parking lots were full every day during COVID with families accessing the internet. A friend in a rural part of Virginia said his local radio station broadcast each day the locations of closed public libraries that would have their internet on during school hours.

Stories like these were the reason then-Commissioner (now Chair) Jessica Rosenworcel urged the Federal Communications Committee to expand access to high-speed internet for all families. She called this issue the Homework Gap—the gap between school-age children who have access to high-speed internet at home and those who don't. As Rosenworcel said, "We have asked students to join a digital classroom, but they literally cannot get there."

As was to be the case with many other pandemic-related issues, the equity gaps for technology access were enormous. The nonprofit organization

All4Ed surveyed schools about the availability of technology during the spring of 2020. They found:

- 34 percent of American Indian/Alaska Native households had no internet access at home, and nearly 16 percent had no computer;
- 36 percent of Americans living in rural areas of the United States had no high-speed internet at home; 14 percent lacked a computer;
- 31 percent of Latino families did not have high-speed internet, and 17 percent had no computer;
- Nearly 31 percent of Black families had no high-speed internet and 17 percent had no computer.[8]

Especially in the early weeks of school closure, students' ability to tune into online education, then, was often entirely dependent on their family's resources. Suddenly every family member was in the same place. Access to devices and to internet connectivity was often limited.

ENGLISH LEARNERS

Astrid Garcia, a student at William & Mary, is also a counselor for a church program that serves immigrant families. She said the abrupt school closure was often very hard for families to navigate. "We served one family who had eight children. They were sharing a one-bedroom apartment with relatives who had three children. That meant eleven kids trying to sign on to school and pay attention to what the teacher was saying, all at the same time."

In most of the families she worked with, the parents spoke little English. Even if they had enough devices and adequate access to the internet, there were challenges just getting their children signed on. Many were unfamiliar with web-based formats like webinars, and the language barrier often made it harder for school personnel to explain how parents could take advantage of these opportunities. "So when younger children had tech problems, they had to depend on older siblings or cousins—themselves sometimes only eleven or twelve years old—to manage everything," Garcia said.

Garcia saw firsthand the importance Spanish-speaking families placed on keeping their children engaged with learning. They made it a priority, even when lost work cut into the family income. The Alexandria, Virginia, public schools had done a good job of making sure the children had computers, Garcia says. But families still had to make sure their children could get online. "They told us that they paid their cable bill first," she said. "Even if they had to come to us with a request for help with food or rent, they paid that bill so their kids could stay online."

Young children from families who spoke little or no English "really struggled," said Garcia of the immigrant families she worked with in Alexandria, Virginia. "The children arrived on the first day of school speaking only Spanish. And while they would previously have been quickly provided services for English language learners, that help wasn't always available online." Everything—from helping these young learners figure out how to log on to assessing the extra help they might need—just took more time. As a result, she said, "Kids spent time officially in school, but not really understanding much about what was going on."

In New York, more than a third (38 percent) of non-English home speakers and a quarter of native Spanish speakers said their child's school had not provided materials in other languages. In California, 24 percent of parents reported getting no help signing on to virtual school. In addition, nearly a third (31 percent) of California parents said their school district was providing no learning materials for English learners.[9]

A report by the General Accounting Office confirmed that English learners and their families faced a special set of challenges. Parents were not always available to help students because they were more likely to be essential workers required to work outside the home. Yet for younger students, some type of adult participation was almost always a requirement to help students get logged on and focused on what they were supposed to be learning. Older children in the family were responsible for caring for younger siblings or working to help support their families, likely due to COVID-19 job losses in their families.

In addition, the more traditional forms of school-family communication, including chatting with parents during school drop-off and pickup times, were no longer available to schools. Some districts tried using Spanish-language television stations to get messages to parents. Others tried to set up hotlines so parents could call and get help figuring out the technology to get their kids logged on.

Because most parents owned a smart phone, teachers sometimes used texting to reach out to parents. While that worked for answers to specific questions, it was less successful as a way to address more complex questions. As a result, English learner students were at times unable to participate in virtual learning.[10]

The biggest hurdles arose when the family's main breadwinner contracted COVID. "These were the families who worked in restaurants or essential retail stores. They went out to get work as day laborers. And sometimes they got sick," Garcia recalled. At that point, things could fall apart. Parents were too sick to make sure their children were up in time to sign on to school. So the children missed one or more days of learning.

Given those challenges, it is not surprising that schools simply lost track of some of their students. Especially in those early weeks, the parents who were most likely to fall out of contact with their school were low-income parents or parents of color.

The US Department of Education highlighted one survey in spring 2020 finding that nearly 30 percent of principals from schools serving "large populations of students of color and students from lower-income households" said they had difficulty reaching some of their students and/or families. In wealthier, predominantly white schools, that number was reduced by more than half to just 14 percent.[11]

STUDENTS WITH DISABILITIES

It was day four of virtual learning for a first-grade class. One of the parents in the class looked at her daughter's screen. And in the array of little rectangular pictures of children, she saw a white board with a message written on it. "I can't learn like this. I have special needs." The child had clearly given up, and the child's parents had obviously also recognized that this style of learning was not going to work for their child.[12]

For many other children with disabilities, virtual learning set back years of educational progress. In Minnesota, Lisa Juliar's son, whose disabilities made it impossible for him to speak, had been on an upward trajectory in school. He was participating in class using his iPad. He had even made presentations in front of the class. He was learning to read.

Then came the school shutdowns. For a student like Juliar's son, moving to an online learning platform was devastating. "His iPad, which was his lifeline and primary means of communication, wouldn't work with the online learning platform," she said. "He was ignored by both the teacher and by other students. No one even acknowledged he was in the room."

Juliar quit her job so she could help her son with school, since he required full-time support. But his frustration increased. Suddenly she was seeing behaviors like screaming or slamming the laptop or grabbing her hair and refusing to let go. "These were not behaviors I had ever seen from him," she said. They were the only way a kid who couldn't speak could express himself.

Because he was not in school, he was cut off from interaction with other students, including some he had become friends with. "All he had left was me, his dog, and our four walls. For months."

As his frustrations mounted, his educational progress regressed. Skills he had acquired were things he could no longer do. He stopped reading and then he stopped wanting his mom to read to him. "We finally just quit," she said.

Many other students with disabilities also stopped attending virtual classes. Some of the best data comes from Connecticut, which conscientiously collected and reported learning data during the pandemic. While attendance was down among all students, a much greater percentage (33 percent) of students with disabilities missed ten or more days of school in 2020–21.[13] Parents of children with IEPs were more than twice as likely than parents of children without IEPs to say that their child was doing little to no remote learning (35 percent, compared with 17 percent), and also to say that virtual learning was not going well for their child (40 percent vs. 19 percent).[14]

In the long term, the pandemic is likely to create further learning gaps for children with disabilities. Because many children missed their regular doctor's checkups, there were also delays in identifying students who might need special education services. The Advocacy Institute, which serves as a resource for individuals with disabilities, noted that the number of young children served by the Individuals with Disabilities Education Act (IDEA) declined by 15 percent over two years. The Institute said the decline was "quite troubling" and could result in lags in service. Early intervention is often key to helping students with disabilities succeed.[15]

During the COVID spring, there wasn't much "school" for Suzann Gallagher's son to attend. "It was roughly an hour a day at the most, but with his ADHD, sitting in front of a computer for even that amount of time was hard."

She describes her son as "reasonably computer savvy," but says the expectations for online learning didn't work at all for him. "To get a kid with ADHD and dyslexia to read all those words on a screen in a short period of time?" From the start of the virtual learning, Suzann says she could see her son's progress eroding.

Over the summer, Fairfax County sent back-and-forth signals about reopening in person. One consequence of the delay was that by the time the family knew for sure that virtual schooling would be the only option for the 2020–2021 school year, it was too late to get her son enrolled in a private school. "That was hard for us because we already knew the fall would be a challenge for him."

Things were in fact harder in the fall. Now a fifth grader, he was expected to manage a series of educational software applications. He was having trouble learning math virtually. With his ADHD, he often struggled to get assignments completed and turned in on time. "The system simply did not work for kids with disabilities," Suzann says.

Other challenges were also magnified as supporting services. Many of the supports that students with disabilities need to be successful essentially disappeared. For example, some students were supposed to receive four hours of therapy daily. That was impossible if the school day was less than four hours long. Remote learning also reduced the effectiveness of special education services that ordinarily require a hands-on or face-to-face approach or specialized equipment that was unavailable at home. Physical therapy or occupational therapy often requires this kind of in-person contact.

A May 2020 survey conducted by an advocacy organization of more than 1,500 families nationwide found that only 20 percent of parents with children with IEPs reported they were receiving all of their services. Twice as many (40 percent) said their children were receiving no services at all.[16]

As districts and schools prepared for the fall of 2020, many initially failed to develop detailed strategies to serve students with disabilities via virtual or hybrid learning. One survey of school district reopening plans found that 12 percent made no mention of students with disabilities at all. There was little detail in many of the other plans. While half (52 percent) called for in-person learning, there were few specifics about what would happen if schools remained virtual.[17]

That proved to be a real problem because students with disabilities were much less likely to remain engaged with school while they were online. In Los Angeles, for example, only about half of students with disabilities completed their online learning assignments. That compared with more than two-thirds of all students.

Teachers knew they did not have the tools they needed to help students during virtual learning. One survey of New York special educators found that 50 percent said they did not have the tools and skills necessary to address the needs of students with disabilities in remote or hybrid learning.[18]

One of the protections offered to students with disabilities under the federal special education law is the Individualized Education Plan, or IEP. This legally binding document spells out educational goals for the student and lays out the special services the child will receive to meet those goals. Once an IEP is signed by both parents and the school, it is considered a contract.

Lisa Juliar had spent enough time negotiating her son's IEP over the years that she knew something was amiss when the district sent her a new version. She was even more concerned when she read what was included. "They had removed educational goals, without my knowledge or consent," she said.

She set up a meeting with the district. Ultimately, it lasted for nine hours. One of the biggest sticking points was her insistence that the IEP include a statement that her son "was unable to learn in the virtual platform." The district representatives would not agree. "We think he was learning," they said. But they could provide no documentation.

Fortunately, Juliar was familiar with a Minnesota law that spelled out how districts provide what are known as "recovery services." (She was familiar with the law because she had helped write it.) The district was, in fact, required not only to "provide the opportunity" for her son to achieve certain education goals but also to keep working to achieve the goals. "Really, what I really wanted," Juliar said, "was the chance for my son to get back to where he was before the pandemic closed schools. I just wanted him to be able to read before he graduated from high school."

There were bright spots. Some students with cognitive disabilities—especially those with attention issues that led them to be easily distractable, and those on the autism spectrum—seem not only to have been successful but to have thrived while learning at home. As one mother of a student diagnosed with attention issues said to me, "The ability to rewind a class lecture or a discussion made it much easier for my son to focus."

FAMILIES' STRESSES PILED UP

The stresses of helping students learn at home were greater when families faced other challenges. Many of Myralyn McCabe's students lived with a family breadwinner who lost a job during the recession. "That meant they would move back home with family to the rez," she said. Sometimes, they were now an hour or even two hours from the school.

As an art teacher, McCabe tried to assemble packets of art supplies so her students could do the projects she assigned in class. But when parents couldn't pick up the packet, her students would be left without any materials for their activity. "Sometimes I'd just tell them to use a cereal box to draw on," she said.

Even families with stable incomes and excellent at-home technology found it hard to manage. In Montgomery County, Maryland, parent Lindsay Dworkin and her husband struggled to figure out how to get their daughter logged on to every class. "The online learning system was almost indecipherable, and it kept changing," she said. "There were individual emails with logins and passwords, websites you had to find and log into through different platforms. There were spreadsheets that attempted to pull it all together.

"One Sunday night, my husband and I sat from 11:30 at night until after 1:00 in the morning, using two computers, just trying to figure out where our daughter was supposed to log in and when."

There wasn't much class time. And classes were "at a different time every day and not even on the hour or the half hour. Instead, class would start at 8:35 or 10:55. And everything happened at a different time every single day."

For supplementary material, parents could log into websites provided by the math and reading curriculum publishers. "Those platforms were, of course, different from the platforms to log into the instruction," she said.

In San Francisco, Spencer and Krista Potter—two parents in professional jobs with two young children—recognized that they were entering a period of at-home schooling "from a position of real privilege." They had jobs with enough work flexibility to allow them to supervise their kindergarten son's online learning (their daughter was in preschool at the time). They already owned devices and had access to high-speed internet.

Even so, helping with schoolwork was "extremely challenging," Spencer said. He and Krista took turns supervising their kindergartener son's learning, alternating with trying to finish their own most important work tasks. But they never felt like they could catch up. Even when they tried to carve out time, they could only eke out about five hours during the work day to focus on their jobs. That meant the rest of their work responsibilities had to be met "in the early morning or late evening when the kids were asleep," he says.

Sarah Johnson, whose oldest daughter was enrolled in kindergarten in March of 2020, says she was later asked how she got through that time. "I told the person who asked that I wasn't even going to answer their question because even now, I can hardly think about it."

There were days when she would get her daughter signed on to school, which would last perhaps forty-five minutes. Then she would have the rest of the day to try to come up with activities. As the spring went on and the two weeks shutdown turned into a closure for the rest of the year, she and the other parents were faced with the sad challenge of coming up with an online kindergarten graduation for their kids. "It's just one of those things that the children look forward to every year, and having it canceled on top of every-thing else was hard to explain."

Throughout the spring, schools worked hard and creatively to make con-nectivity available. In many districts school buses equipped with Wi-Fi were deployed to neighborhoods with little or no connectivity. The *Texas Tribune* described how the program worked in Austin: "Students learned which spots in their homes were within Wi-Fi reach. Parents called bus drivers and asked them to please move the bus a few feet closer or shift a bit to the left so their child's school-provided laptop could catch the signal. Some parents packed sandwich lunches and spent hours in the car with their kids parked next to what was a hulking yellow internet router."[19]

But sometimes parents who *thought* they had high-speed internet con-nectivity discovered that it wasn't adequate. The Indianapolis public schools surveyed parents over the summer. Even when a family had a broadband con-nection, it often could not support two or three students in full-time school, especially if a parent was working at home.

A STUDENT'S STORY OF A TECH FAILURE

Sometimes, it was the school's infrastructure that simply didn't work. Probably the most publicized case of a technology meltdown occurred in Virginia's Fairfax County Public Schools (FCPS). The district has long held a reputation for being a national education leader. FCPS is often compared to a battleship—the system is big (at 189,000 students, one of the largest districts in the nation) and powerful.

But big ships turn slowly. So it was not surprising that the school system took a slow and deliberate approach after Virginia governor Ralph Northam announced on March 23, 2020, that all schools in the Commonwealth would be closed for the remainder of the school year. After shutting schools, FCPS waited for four weeks—including a week of spring break—before going online.

Its reputation, coupled with the fact that the district's hometown newspaper is the *Washington Post*, almost guaranteed that national news would cover the implosion of virtual learning on the first day students could sign back on. I spoke with one of these students, who provided an unvarnished look at the frustration that students felt when they tried to resume their learning.

As a second-semester senior, Leia Surovell didn't have a lot of formal school left, but Advanced Placement tests loomed. "I like to be academically engaged," Leia said. "When I was a kid, I didn't like summer because I'd get really bored." Getting back to an actual class felt like getting back to normal.

First out of the gate was Leia's favorite class, AP Environmental Science, taught by a favorite teacher. To commemorate the "first day of school" vibe, and to celebrate the fact that "I always learned something in that class," Leia dressed in nice clothes "for the first time in weeks."

The school had sent students information on how to log on. There was no password required for entry into any individual class, and students were free to choose their own screen names, which guaranteed anonymity in the chat room.

And about thirty minutes into a lesson on plate tectonics, those anonymous students in the chat room took over. They filled the chat with homophobic and racist slurs, including using the n-word. "The teacher had no way to close anyone out of the chat," Leia said. "All he could do was to stop class or to press on. I admire him for sticking it out, but at the same time it was really hard to watch."

The behavior was not confined to one class. "I heard from a friend in an English class taught by an openly gay Black English teacher, where people sent openly racist and homophobic messages in the chat. And my younger sister was in an entry-level German class," Surovell says. There, the chat room included students who adopted screen names like "I Love Adolf Hitler" and "Oven Survivor #2."

Students were horrified. And they couldn't believe that after a month of reading news stories about how college classes had been "Zoom Bombed" by students posting pornographic or derogatory messages that Fairfax County had not set up security procedures to ensure that the only students who entered an online class were entitled to be there.

Leia and their friends were "appalled." They reported their concerns to the principal. They contacted the superintendent. And then, when it felt like the school system was "incapable of stopping this behavior," they reached out to the *Washington Post.*

Because of earlier concerns about racist, homophobic, and antisemitic comments, Leia had worked with the school's leadership class to sponsor a Diversity Week at their school. It was scheduled for the week schools were closed, and it was never rescheduled.

Leia's experience was hardly unique. Across the system, teachers, parents, and students reported stories of harassment and bad behavior from students who hid behind the anonymity of a fake name.

When fifty thousand students tried to log in to the online learning platform simultaneously, the system simply couldn't handle the traffic. In a *Washington Post* interview, Blackboard's chief product officer Tim Tomlinson said that neither the company nor FCPS ever considered running a capacity test, since it was "standard practice" not to.[20] Given the obstructive behavior of some students, it may have been fortunate that not everyone could even log on.

A school system tweet acknowledged that "FCPS Blackboard 24–7 Learning is currently experiencing login issues across the system." The second day of virtual learning was not much more successful. After two days, the school system shut down online learning for the remainder of the week.

Families with younger children had bigger challenges when the Fairfax County virtual school finally started. The Geller-Cheney kids were in kindergarten, third grade, and fifth grade. They all had to log in to the county's Blackboard system every day, but they also had to log in to some individual classes. There was a separate login for Spanish. There was a separate login for music, except when it didn't work and then there was a different login. While the fifth grader was able to handle all of that pretty easily, their kindergartener daughter "was reading, kind of, but not well enough to navigate on a computer," Geller said. "If she got one thing wrong, the link wouldn't work. But then again, the links didn't work a lot of the time anyway." All of that meant that parents had to be pretty hands-on getting the kids started every day or whenever they changed classes.

They initially thought their third-grade son, who has ADHD, was managing fairly well. It was not long, however, before they discovered that he had learned how to find YouTube and the games on his school-issued computer. "So one of us had to sit with him just to make sure he was doing school and not just messing around."

Even then, Rebecca knew that he sometimes managed to get off track. "That was when the teacher would text me and say, 'Maybe you should check on what he's doing because he is not paying attention to what we're doing in class.'" Impulse control, of course, is one of the issues that kids with ADHD have to deal with. "It wasn't that he couldn't do the work," she said. "It was that he sometimes just didn't."

(The other musical challenge for the family was unrelated to technology. In Fairfax County, third grade is when students learn to play the recorder. Any parent who has ever lived through that music unit will understand that it really didn't matter how many rooms your house had—it was nearly impossible for a parent to get far enough away.)

HOW SOME SCHOOLS ADAPTED
TO VIRTUAL LEARNING

There were some schools and districts that had laid the groundwork for a successful transition to virtual learning. Chapter 7 tells the story of how the Kyrene School District in Tempe, Arizona, transformed its already innovative SPARK school into a virtual school that meet the needs of families and educators.

Another success story came out of a group of schools in center-west Fairfax County. While the district as a whole struggled with the transition to virtual learning, the Chantilly Pyramid had an established 1:1 computer device program that had been providing all students in the pyramid (six elementary schools, two middle schools, and one high school) with devices since the 2017–2018 school year.

The program, known as FCPSOn, was designed to make technology integration a central part of each student's learning. Teachers received professional development in how they could use technology to transform their instruction. Students from second grade up were allowed to take their devices home.

If there was anywhere in the country where the transition to virtual learning should have been smooth, it was here. And, compared with many other school districts, and even with other parts of the county, things were easier. But there were still problems.

Jennifer and Matt McNerney are the parents of two students: a daughter who was in seventh grade and a son who was in fourth grade when schools closed down. "They were both used to using their laptop every day, and to bringing their laptop home every day," Matt said.

Jennifer worked from home, and during the pandemic, Matt was also able to work at home. In addition to the school-provided technology, the family owned "more devices than you could shake a stick at," Matt said.

In other words, "We were as ready for distance learning as a family could be."

And even with all that support and training, the switch to virtual learning was rocky at best. Even in the Chantilly area, "where our students were used to using Blackboard," Jennifer McNerney said, there were glitches. Students couldn't sign on. When they did sign on, they sometimes got kicked off. Teachers had trouble accessing the platform. "One of our son's teachers lived so far out that her internet connection was unstable," Jennifer said.

Their daughter took the technology issues in stride. But their son had more trouble adapting. He was worried that his teacher might not know he was trying to sign on. He'd ask questions like, "What am I missing? Am I going to get in trouble?"

His parents were reassuring. "It's not your fault," they'd repeat. "We're all going to be in survival mode, and we will get through this."

And eventually the schools did get things up and running successfully. But after the technology platform was stabilized, there were still teachers who struggled to use technology in their lessons. "Some teachers just hadn't been trained in how to use technology," Jennifer said.

In classes where teachers had a better handle on the instructional component, not all students were able to get online. "A significant amount of class time was spent with teachers helping kids troubleshoot technology issues," Jennifer said. "The teachers were not particularly well equipped to do that, and it was not very interesting for the students who had already figured out how to get online."

SOME FAMILIES DROPPED OUT

Parents and students, in a preview of what would happen on a larger scale during the 2020–2021 school year, found ways to encourage their kids to learn even when they weren't officially "in school."

Elena Guarinello and Jessica Latterman confronted daily challenges of "coming through this portal for this class and that portal for that class" to get their Montgomery County, Maryland, second grader signed into her reading or math classes, Elena recalled.

But with only an hour of online class on most days, and with one day when there was no class at all, "School did not factor a great deal into our lives in spring 2020." Their daughter had the time for more leisure reading and activities like drawing that she enjoyed. "Once we knew the school closure was not going to be just two weeks, our attitude was, 'Well, we're just going to get to June.'"

When it became clear that in-person school was not going to happen for the remainder of the school year, said Margaret Millar, "for the most part we abandoned school. With our general anxiety about a global pandemic, not having to worry about our son's experience in a school he didn't like was a relief. Our goal was just to get through to the end of the year."

They read books. They planned activities. They felt incredibly fortunate that both of them could work from home. "Essentially, we just cobbled together each day."

The Christensen family was clear from the start that they would not do virtual school when the Boulder, Colorado, schools went online.

Over the course of the spring, Nicole talked with a number of friends whose children were struggling with online learning. She reported that they "felt a tremendous amount of pressure to keep their kids in this structure that didn't really work for anybody."

Teachers sent home materials. "They were doing more than ever," Nicole says. But the whole structure of online just wasn't working for many students.

So the family "legitimately quit school." Their two daughters, one in pre-school, didn't stop learning, however. There was a schedule for every day. The schedule included chances for the children to play outside and to do projects. "But we just weren't stressed about a style of learning that we knew would never work for us."

STUDENTS DISAPPEARED

They had plenty of company. As early as April, the *New York Times* reported that "more students than ever are missing class—not logging on, not checking in or not completing assignments. The absence rate appears particularly high in schools with many low-income students, whose access to home computers and internet connections can be spotty. Some teachers report that fewer than half of their students are regularly participating."[21]

Even before the pandemic, an estimated one in six students was chronically absent from school (defined as missing 10 percent or more of all school days).[22] But when the pandemic hit, that number soared. And the lowest attendance rates to "follow the contours of poverty," said Hedy Chang, Attendance Works founder and executive director. "For both urban and rural areas where there [were] pockets of poverty, you [saw] higher levels of chronic absence."[23]

Six months into the pandemic, the nonprofit organization Bellwether Education Partners estimated that as many as three million children had experienced minimal or no contact with education since schools had closed.[24]

Myralyn McCabe said she noticed a drop-off in student attendance the longer school remained virtual. "Kids started out being there every day. Then they'd sign off early. Or they'd show up late. Then they stopped coming at all."

The Los Angeles Unified School District's attendance problems were likely no worse than many other urban districts, but they did have better data. The district took a comprehensive look at student engagement after schools closed in March. They found that only 60 percent of secondary students were active each day, and that activities, including posting on message boards, was "much lower."[25] The report, which used the district's Schoology platform to keep track of which students logged in to class, found that English learners, students with disabilities, students experiencing homelessness, and students in foster care in middle and high school were all less likely than their peers to log in. Between 6 and 10 percent of students in those subgroups did not log in at all from March through May.

And despite teachers' best efforts to reach out to absent students, many simply had no way to contact families. Although a majority of teachers nationwide (59 percent) said they could contact all or nearly all their students and families, that access was not evenly distributed across schools and student populations. Fewer than half (47 percent) of secondary school teachers and teachers in high poverty schools (49 percent) were able to communicate with all or most of their students.[26]

Near the end of May, when most students in the United States would normally have been in school, the US Census Bureau found that nearly 93 percent of households with school-age children reported that their children were engaged in some form of "distance learning."[27] But the type of distance learning they were doing varied dramatically by family income.

In households with incomes of $100,000 or more, 85.8 percent of people with children told the Census Bureau they were using online resources. But only 65.8 percent of families with less than $50,000 were using online resources. Instead, they were relying on learning packets sent home by the school.[28]

In other words, it was not that lower-income students *wouldn't* log in to their classes every day. It was that they *couldn't*. "The schoolhouse and the school bus are now a computer and Wi-Fi," said Cara McClellan, assistant counsel for the NAACP's Legal Defense and Educational Fund. "In some districts, we're talking about a third of Black students who are not able to access their education."[29]

It wasn't just a lack of internet access that made it hard for students to learn at home. Often, students lacked even the most basic learning tools—pencils, rulers, and markers. In Oakland, the organization Oakland Promise, which is designed to encourage students to attend postsecondary education, distributed more than six thousand kits containing some of the supplies students would need for virtual schooling. Kits included pencils and a pencil sharpener, crayons, a whiteboard, markers, and other basic supplies that would make it easier to do their assignments.

In March, Congress passed what would be the first of three major COVID relief packages. The Coronavirus Aid, Relief, and Economic Security (CARES) Act included $13.2 billion for state education departments and local school districts through the Elementary and Secondary School Emergency Relief Fund (ESSER) Fund. Purchasing computers and wireless connective devices were both allowable ESSER expenditures.

HOW DID REMOTE LEARNING WORK? NOT WELL

One of the toughest lessons to learn after kids went back to school was this: while nearly every student had some learning loss, those who needed direct instruction and support from a teacher the most—low-income students, English learners, students with disabilities, and Black and Brown students— had the most dramatic losses. As chapter 4 documents, pandemic-related school closures widened the already substantial learning gap.

Students who were already behind in March, 2020, saw exponential growth in the gap between their performance and that of their peers who started much closer to grade level. Virginia's Department of Education found that after one semester of at-home learning, 36 percent of low-income kindergarteners and nearly half (49 percent) of kindergarten English learners were at high risk of reading failure. Black students, students with disabilities, and Latino students were similarly struggling.[30]

Virginia's Standards of Learning tests given at the end of the 2020–21 school year showed marked declines for all students. For students of color, the declines were even more worrisome. Black students saw scores on the math test drop from a pass rate of 70 percent in 2019 to a pass rate of 34 percent in 2021. English language learners saw passing rates in math drop from 59 percent to 21 percent.[31]

And as researchers from The Hamilton Project noted, learning gaps do not go away by themselves. "Students who fall behind grade-level material tend to stay behind. When these students miss developing crucial foundational skills, they can have major difficulties in subsequent learning tasks, which worsens the gap between them and their grade-level peers as they move from one grade to the next. This persistent mismatch between the learning needs of students and what classroom instruction delivers can seriously undermine students' chances of success in the workforce and beyond," researchers from the project noted.[32]

STATES AND DISTRICTS TRY TO DEAL WITH LEARNING CHALLENGES

Schools began adjusting to the painful reality that even the most well-intentioned students might not be able to get to class. In most districts, teachers provided instruction to the students who had devices and could log on. But many students could not. During the early weeks, teachers reviewed concepts they had already taught. But by mid-April, when some schools still had six to eight weeks of school on their calendar, school districts made hard choices.

The experience of families in this chapter—that there simply wasn't all that much "school" during virtual school—was pretty common. The US Department of Education reported that in May 2020, only 15 percent of districts expected elementary school students to receive instruction for more than four hours a day during virtual learning. The vast majority—85 percent—were providing students at least one hour per day less than the pre-pandemic normal average of five hours of instructional time a day. In nearly a fifth of districts surveyed (17 percent), the instruction students did receive in spring 2020 was designed not to teach new skills and understanding, but to review what had already been taught. They were caught in a sort of pandemic holding pattern.[33]

Across the country, teachers were not required to take attendance for the remainder of the 2020 school year. National data collected by McKinsey & Company found that only 60 percent of low-income, and 60 to 70 percent of Black and Hispanic students, logged in regularly to their online classes. For their more affluent peers, the number was closer to 90 percent.[34]

A RAND study found that nearly all teachers—80 percent—reported requiring students to complete assigned learning activities. Only one-third said they were issuing a letter grade for what students did. Roughly one in five—17 percent—said they kept track of whether students completed an assignment but provided no feedback or grade for the students' work.[35]

Many schools decided to forgo traditional grading for the last weeks of the year and switched to a pass-fail system. States encouraged schools not to penalize students who were unable to sign on.

Five of the state's six largest districts in California followed state guidance that students should be "held harmless"—in other words, that they should not receive a worse grade than they were on track to earn before schools shut down. Los Angeles Unified, San Diego Unified, and Fresno Unified adopted hold harmless policies. Long Beach Unified switched to a pass/fail or credit/ no credit grading system. San Francisco Unified considered awarding all students As for the last marking period.

Of the largest California school districts, only Elk Grove Unified maintained its regular grading system.[36] Both the University of California and the California State University systems announced they would recognize pass/ fail or credit/no credit grades.

Other states waived some graduation requirements. Arizona, Idaho, Illinois, Kansas, Ohio, Oregon, Mississippi, Virginia, and Wisconsin. These included minimum attendance hours, end-of-course examinations, and even some mandated courses. Local districts were allowed to make decisions about whether students met the requirements for high school graduation.[37]

Illinois waived other requirements such as teacher and principal evaluations, according to state board of education chair Darren Reisberg. Because some teachers were not able to complete their student teaching, the state "set up a coaching-mentoring program for new teachers who would enter the profession in the fall of 2020. We tried to ensure that they had additional support."

Because most states and districts had waived their graduation requirements, there was actually a small uptick in the graduation rate for that year. But in the fall, many fewer of these students entered college. The National Student Clearinghouse, which tracks postsecondary enrollment, noted that overall, college enrollment dropped by 3.6 percent. The sharpest declines were in community colleges, which often serve low-income students. Of the high school students who earned a high school diploma in the spring, more than 327,500 fewer enrolled in college than high school graduates from the Class of 2019. The Clearinghouse called that decline "unprecedented."[38]

Hardest hit, of course, were the students who most needed postsecondary education to prepare for a well-paying job. "The impact of the pandemic seems to be disproportionately affecting disadvantaged students by keeping them out of college," said Doug Shapiro, executive director of the National Student Clearinghouse Research Center. "Community colleges and freshmen saw the steepest drops in enrollment, while the declines among four-year colleges and continuing undergraduates were generally much smaller.[39]

"Looking through the additional lens of 2020 high school graduates, we observe an even sharper picture, as the immediate college enrollments of those from high-poverty, low-income, and urban high schools have been hit the hardest. The enrollment gaps appear to be widening because of COVID-19 and the recession."

GRANDPARENTS PLAYED A KEY ROLE

I had a standard set of questions I asked parents when I interviewed them for this book. I did not include a question about grandparents. But I was surprised that, over and over, parents brought up the help they had received from their own parents as essential to getting their kids through school closures.

Spencer Potter's mom is a retired elementary school teacher, and even though she lived across the country from his family, she wanted to provide support. "How can I help from a distance?" she asked.

She'd buy a packet of books and send them to her grandson, keeping a duplicate set for herself. Then on scheduled Face Time calls, the two of them would read together. She'd read a page. Then he'd read a page. Or they'd read a page together. "It gave us some time when we could do other things," Spencer said. "We knew he was happy and learning."

Because of that constant engagement with print, their son came out of the pandemic "reading well above grade level," Potter says. "I give a lot of credit for that to his grandmother."

Some families simply decamped and temporarily took up residence with extended family. At the end of the COVID spring, Margaret and Tom Millar were worn out. They loaded the family in the car and drove straight to his parents' house. It was on a beach, which meant there would be places for the kids to safely play outdoors. But even more important, there would be other adults to pick up some of the responsibilities. "I felt we showed up essentially broken on their doorstep," Margaret said. "They took us in, fed us meatloaf, and spent time with our kids."

Myralyn McCabe relied on her husband's mom for support while she was teaching. Family is important in the Navajo culture. "Three days a week, my son would go to her house," she said. "But it was stressful for my son's grandmother if the internet would go out or Zoom would crash or there would be some tech glitch. She tried to stockpile things my son could do in case the technology didn't work."

SCHOOL LUNCH PROGRAM AS A MODEL

That is not to say schools did not make a difference. In Mississippi, State Superintendent of Education Carey Wright worked with the state's medical community to expand telehealth and teletherapy for students statewide, including those in rural areas.[40] In 2022, Deputy Secretary of Education Cindy Marten said to the Council of Great City Schools that in many places, schools "were the largest relief effort in our communities."[41]

From the start, schools, states, and the Department of Agriculture (USDA) were determined to make it easy to provide children with the food that was a lifeline for so many low-income families. The biggest potential obstacle? The school lunch program is largely funded with federal funds, and like other federal programs is subject to a host of rules and regulations. But Congress quickly gave USDA the authority to be more flexible, and perhaps because Agriculture Secretary Sonny Perdue was a former governor, the USDA listened to states and localities. Instead of requiring state-by-state applications for rule changes, the USDA issued blanket waivers. By March 26, the first waivers were in place.

States and districts responded. "From March of 2020 through the end of the year, school nutrition efforts were as significant as the remote learning in our schools," says Darren Reisberg, chair of the Illinois State Board of Education. "The priority initially was really keeping families alive."

School buildings were closed, but districts repurposed their school buses to transport and distribute food. To reduce contact time for staff, some districts offered families up to one week of meals at a time. Because job losses in the pandemic led to rising rates of hunger for adults as well as children, many school lunch programs provided meals to adults at low or no cost. Other districts partnered with local food banks or food pantries to provide families with one-stop food distribution.

In St. Paul, Minnesota, 70 percent of the thirty-six thousand students were eligible for free and reduced lunch. For many of the families, especially those where the main wage earner had been laid off in the pandemic, the breakfasts and lunches were the only source of food for the children.

Before the end of March, the school system had developed a plan to deliver food to all students in the district. Bus drivers drove their regular routes and families could receive a week's worth of food.[42]

THE END OF THE SCHOOL YEAR

On March 17, Kansas governor Laura Kelly announced that classes in the state would not resume until fall.[43] The state's school calendar meant that schools in Kansas closed earlier and would reopen earlier than in most parts of the United States. On May 20, the CDC issued its first guidance document on how to safely reopen schools. It included this advice for schools: "Schools that are currently closed, remain closed. E-learning or distance learning opportunities should be provided for all students. Support provision of student services such as a school meal programs as feasible."[44]

Ultimately, all but two states and the District of Columbia announced their decision to close all schools for the remainder of the school year. Montana and Wyoming deferred to local school districts, and as a practical matter their schools remained closed. The Department of Defense schools and schools in four territories also announced they would not reopen for the remainder of the school year.

Class trips and athletic competitions and proms were all canceled. Senior yearbook signing day, the band trip, the spring musical? All canceled. Graduations turned into outdoor car parades, virtual celebrations, or outdoor ceremonies held in parking lots, on beaches, or in parks. The high school class that had been born just after the September 11 attacks rounded out their high school career with a senior year that just . . . stopped.

Meanwhile, families felt increasingly isolated as they waited to hear what school might look like for their children in the next school year. "There was no support for families from either the federal or the state government, even in arguably the most progressive jurisdiction in the country," Spencer Potter said about the schools in his home town of San Francisco. "When it comes down to it, the pandemic made me realize that families are fundamentally on our own."

CHAPTER 3

THE PERMANENT "TEMPORARY" SCHOOL CLOSURES

We are now confronted by insurmountable opportunities.

—Walt Kelly, *Pogo*

COVID did not create disparities in education. COVID exposed and then amplified the inequities that have existed in the public school system for generations. Issues of poverty, race, disability, and language left many students behind the starting line when schools closed in 2020.

Parents did not spend the spring of 2020 reading research studies. But their lived experience confirmed what experts were saying. At the end of that first long spring of school closures, Education Trust polled parents in several states. Nearly nine out of ten reported feeling worried that their children were falling behind academically. And nearly eight in ten said their children were experiencing heightened stress levels.[1]

For the students who were already behind when the schools closed in the spring, learning gaps grew exponentially over the next six months. An analysis by McKinzie & Company found that students, on average, started the 2020–2021 school about three months behind where they would have ordinarily been in mathematics. Students of color were about three to five months behind in learning; white students were about one to three months behind.[2]

Early in the pandemic, some experts were already sounding alarms about the harmful effects of long-term virtual schooling. Chad Aldeman, the policy director for the Georgetown Edunomics Lab, wrote a series of articles for the website *The 74* in which he looked at past educational disruptions and made predictions about how school closures would affect the children enrolled in school during COVID.

35

Lost learning time, he predicted in a later interview for this book, would likely translate into lost learning, and the losses were likely to be large. Learning losses would be greater in math. Kids from low-income families would suffer more. The longest-lasting impact was likely to be felt by the youngest learners. "It was pretty hard to watch as nearly all of my predictions in that article started coming true."

A group of scholars at the Brookings Institution warned that the consequences of school closures would be long lasting. "Some modeling suggests that the loss of learning during the extraordinary systemic crisis of World War II still had negative impact on former students' lives some 40 years later. For whole societies closing down education today, there will likely be significant consequences tomorrow."[3]

But for a variety of reasons, some motivated by well-intentioned caution and some by politics, schools closed for weeks or even months. School officials were more aware of the challenges of remote learning than anyone. Starting almost the day schools were closed in March, they began discussing how and when reopening could occur. Mostly they laid out specific actions: encourage mask wearing, for example, or find ways to maintain social distances.

Schools did make those adjustments. They bought plexiglass by the acre and hand sanitizer by the gallon. They bought expensive (and ultimately, as it turned out, not very effective) air purifiers. When they could find masks (because of supply chain issues again), they purchased them.

But in fact, all of those actions could not really fix the problem. Reopening schools was not something the schools could manage on their own. Whether students and teachers could safely return to school buildings depended much more on how widespread the coronavirus was throughout the community at large.

There were no vaccines, and the best estimates from health experts were that it would take eighteen to twenty-four months before a vaccine could be developed. One of those experts, Dr. Michael Osterholm, director of the Center for Infectious Disease Research and Policy at the University of Minnesota, offered this gloomy prediction in March of 2020: "Our leaders need to begin by stating a number of hard truths about our situation. The first is that no matter what we do at this stage, numerous hospitals in the United States will be overrun. Many people, including health care workers, will get sick and some will die. And the economy will tank. It's too late to change any of this now."[4]

There was not enough personal protective equipment to ensure that even hospital workers, let alone teachers and school principals, could have masks. While there was a growing understanding that COVID testing could help people determine whether they should isolate themselves, the chemicals required to produce the tests were in short supply. "Trying to get these materials is not about dollars and cents; it's about physics," Osterholm said. "You can't just buy these things. It takes time to make them." Even if there had been tests available, one of the most challenging characteristics of this virus was that people who contracted it often showed no symptoms for several days.

Yet on July 23, the CDC revised its guidance to schools. While some schools had decided on in-school screenings for students as a way to reopen safely, the CDC recommended against that practice. The document also made a compelling case for keeping students in school if possible.

Here are the ways that the CDC said a two-week closure would affect the health of the community, families, and schools:

- Impact on disease
  - Modeling data for other respiratory infections where children have higher disease impacts suggests that early short-term closures are not impactful in terms of overall transmission.
  - Social mixing may still occur outside of school with less ability to monitor, especially among older students.
  - Will increase risk to older adults or those with co-morbidities, as almost 40 percent of US grandparents provide childcare. School closures will likely increase this percentage.
- Impact on families
  - Key services are interrupted for students (e.g., meals, other social, physical health, mental health services, and after school programs).
  - Economic impact for families because of the costs of childcare and lost wages. There may be a loss of productivity even for parents who are able to telework.
  - Some families may not be able to have students participate in distance learning (e.g., no computers, internet access issues) even if provided by the school.
- Impact on schools
  - Potential academic impact because of the disruption to the continuity of learning.[5]

On masks, the CDC equivocated, "While cloth face coverings are strongly encouraged to reduce the spread of COVID-19, CDC recognizes there are specific instances when wearing a cloth face covering may not be feasible."

Despite this CDC guidance, however, the federal approach was still to leave decisions about school reopenings to states, counties, and cities. Most elected officials were faced with the difficult balancing act of getting people back to work while also keeping down the spread of the virus. As early as May 2020, states began relaxing the strict rules closing retail establishments, restaurants, and bars. As one mayor told me during the spring of 2020, "Our long-term planning right now is looking at the week *after* next."

Policy makers were making important decisions without the information that public health officials call "surveillance" information: They didn't know how many people were infected with the virus, and they didn't know where those who had COVID were located. In the absence of that information, there was no way to determine when the coronavirus numbers in a particular community had reached a tipping point.

The solution should have been to keep the spread of the virus in the community surrounding the schools to the lowest possible level. That was the policy adopted in most European countries. From the earliest days of the pandemic, the priority was to keep schools open.

"The school environment, in our perception, is still quite a controlled environment," Steven Van Gucht, the head of viral diseases at Sciensano, Belgium's national public health institute, told the *Washington Post* in September of 2020. "We think it's better to have schools open than to send kids home, have them meet on the street and give them more opportunities to spread the virus."[6]

As chapter 1 laid out, European schools were closed for much less time.

Reopening of schools for all students in countries with low community transmission (Denmark and Norway) did not result in a significant increase in the growth rate of COVID-19 cases.[7]

Watching the European response to COVID, writer German Lopez said, "If you want to reopen schools this fall, then you need to get the spread of Covid-19 down, as close to zero as possible, this summer. And that means opting not to reopen—possibly at all and definitely not at full capacity—restaurants, bars, nightclubs, or other places that will lead to significantly more coronavirus spread but have less value to society than schools." In no state did the governor say, "We are going to take things a little more slowly with reopening so that we can be sure our kids are back in school next fall."

By the traditional September opening day of school, nearly all states had reopened bars and restaurants, although often at reduced hours or with seating limitations. But the schools? For many students, school effectively did not reopen for an entire year.

As pediatrician Jennifer P. Nuzzo and epidemiologist Joshua M. Sharfstein said in a *New York Times* opinion piece, "The way states lifted social distancing restrictions imposed to fight the coronavirus sadly demonstrates our priorities. Officials let bars, restaurants and gyms open, despite warnings from public health experts that these environments pose the greatest risk for spreading the disease."[8]

Superintendents and school boards had no control over whether tanning salons were open. But they did have to make tough decisions about the things they *could* control. Should schools be reopened for in-person learning, or should virtual learning continue? Should masks be required? How far apart should desks be place so the virus wouldn't spread? Could children eat lunch inside?

"Because of the lack of guidance at the national level, school boards and superintendents were left to their own devices," recalled Dan Domenech, the executive director of AASA, the School Superintendents Association. "In one community, schools were open. In the school district next door, they were closed. In a third, schools were open, but everyone had to be masked. Every school district had a different approach."

There was simply no consensus about whether, when, and how to reopen schools. In August of 2020, a Pew Research poll found that any school leader who wanted to "listen to what parents say" about school reopening would not have heard a clear message. Among the parents whose children were scheduled to attend an elementary, middle, or high school, 32 percent said they thought their child's school should provide online instruction five days a week. Nearly the same number (34 percent) said schools should offer a hybrid mix, with students spending some time in the school building and some time learning virtually. A smaller but not insignificant number of parents (23 percent) said schools should offer in-person instruction five days a week.[9]

As the pandemic stretched on, response to COVID divided strikingly along partisan lines. It was, said Drew Altman, president and CEO of the Kaiser Family Foundation, "as if the country has both red and blue pandemics. When that happened, the public's willingness to prevent the spread of the virus substantially collapsed across red America."

For example, 36 percent of Republicans or Republican-leaning independents supported a return to full-time in-person schooling, while only 6 percent of Democrats or Democratic-leaning independents did. Conversely, while 41 percent of Democrats wanted schools to focus on offering full-time virtual learning, just 13 percent of Republicans did.

When they were asked what factors should weigh most heavily in a school's decision to reopen, the partisan differences continued. More than four out of five Democrats said the risk to students (82 percent) or to teachers (81 percent) should be given a great deal of consideration. Republican numbers were less than half that (37 percent and 35 percent). On the other hand, Republicans said schools should focus on whether students were falling behind academically (61 percent vs. 36 percent of Democrats) or because their parents could not work if their children were at home (56 percent vs. 43 percent).[10]

In that challenging atmosphere, schools spent the summer simultaneously trying to plan for an in-person and a virtual opening. Absent clear health policy guidance, and in the face of a constantly adapting virus, schools were unable to send parents a clear message about whether they would reopen in the fall. They weren't equivocating. They simply didn't know.

Teacher organizations soon made it clear where they stood. In July, the American Federation of Teachers (AFT) adopted a resolution called Safely Reopening Schools. It included this language:

> RESOLVED, that in the fight to ensure the safety and health of American Federation of Teachers' members, our students and our communities, we will use every action and tool available to us from serving on state and local reopening committees to filing grievances, lawsuits and other actions against unsafe and unsound plans or the faulty implementation of plans. Nothing is off the table when it comes to the safety and health of those we represent and those we serve, including supporting local and/or state affiliate safety strikes on a case-by-case basis as a last resort.[11]

Randi Weingarten, president of the American Federation of Teachers, came down clearly on the side of keeping schools closed in her speech to the convention. Echoing the language of the resolution, she said, "If authorities don't protect the safety and health of those we represent and those we serve . . . nothing is off the table—not advocacy or protests, negotiations, grievances or lawsuits, or, if necessary and authorized by a local union, as a last resort, safety strikes."

Many school systems reached out to parents with options for what they wanted in the fall. Were they comfortable sending their children back to school in person? Did they want a fully virtual start to school? Or should there be some sort of hybrid?

But in district after district, as the date for reopening would come closer, the decision would be put off again. Fairfax County parent Margaret Millar said, "It began to feel a lot like Lucy and the football. Just when you thought you'd get an answer, the deadline changed again."

In the last three weeks of August, there was a big shift back to all-virtual schooling all across the country. The website Burbio, which tracked school closures and reopenings, noted the last-minute change. "We have seen a dramatic shift to online only learning in the past three weeks," said Burbio cofounder Julie Roche in a news release. "Large districts such as Chicago, and Sun Belt cities such as Houston and Miami along with large suburban districts such as Fairfax County Virginia were all setting plans to return with in-person learning and shifted to fully remote."[12]

Between early August and Labor Day, Burbio reported a 10 percent increase in the number of school districts that were planning to open virtually.

That included two-thirds of the nation's two hundred largest districts and 62 percent of US K–12 students.

"There really was a lot of optimism in the summer of 2020 that schools could reopen in the fall," said Dan Domenech of AASA. "Then along came [the] Delta [variant]—and that threw all those plans out the window. Some districts did open, but by the end of September, many of them shut down."

Given the continuing rise in the numbers of COVID cases and the absence of effective preventive vaccines or effective treatment for those who did get sick, the realistic option probably always was that most schools would open remotely. Yet there was little focus during the summer on helping teachers be better prepared for teaching virtually.

"There was a lot of magical thinking that went on in the summer of 2020," said Dan Goldhaber, an education researcher with the American Institutes for Research and a Seattle-area parent. Perhaps, he speculated, that was the reason "the schools were really ill-prepared to make remote instruction a quality experience."

After a virtual start, schools began returning to in-person learning in early November, when the number of all-virtual schools fell to 37 percent. Then a combination of rising COVID rates and fears of an uptick in infections following holiday travel led a number of schools to return to online learning. By early January, 55 percent of students were in virtual-only schools. The entire state of Rhode Island, as well as suburban districts in the Northeast and Midwest, announced they would not reopen for in-person learning until at least February.

Figure 3.1 shows how the schools fluctuated between in-person and virtual schooling during the first half of the school year using data collected by the website Burbio.

These on-again-off-again school closures were difficult for families to accommodate. Parents I spoke to in writing this book all described feeling like they were constantly on a seesaw. They were exhausted.

And no wonder. The evidence came from the Labor Department's Time Use Survey, which takes an annual look at how Americans are spending their time. In 2020, the survey found that the parents who felt they were juggling many responsibilities . . . were, in fact, juggling many responsibilities.

When workers moved home, children still needed care. In addition to direct care—supervising meals, reading aloud—parents watched their kids while doing other things. This multitasking is called "secondary child care," and pandemic parents did a lot of it. The survey found that mothers spent seven hours a day in secondary child care and at least another hour in direct care (fathers spent 2.5 hours less).[13]

So in addition to working eight hours, mothers provided eight *more* hours of child care. When the 2020–2021 school year opened, families were

2020/2021 SCHOOL YEAR IN REVIEW

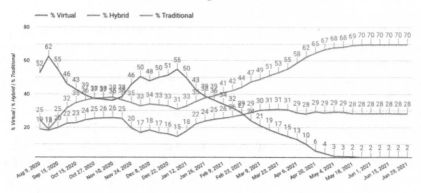

US K-12 Learning Mode Trends

Figure 3.1. 2020/2021 school year in review
Source: Burbio

suddenly facing the grim realization that they might be in the untenable situation of working and learning at home for a very long time. Increasingly, women in the labor force decided they simply could not do a good job of being both a parent and an employee.

One reason is that the hours children spend in school are essential to how many families arrange their work lives. The complicated reality is that while parents do not see schools as day care providers for their children, they nonetheless include the hours children are in school as part of the strategy for ensuring their kids are safe and supervised. Because that in turn is what allows them to do their own work.

Spencer Potter is the son of a teacher. He understands that school and childcare are very different. And yet, he says, "What I really want the school board to appreciate and acknowledge is the dual role that they play. Our whole work-life structure is premised on the fact that schools also care for our kids. That's part of the public trust that we place in schools. They provide a safe place for kids."

As parent Kwame B. said, "Parents can wear multiple hats. But they can't wear multiple hats well. That impacts them on an emotional and mental level and therefore also impacts the kids and their families on an emotional and mental level."

Jenny Poon, the CRPE researcher who studied pod learning, points out that parents didn't initially *choose* to depend on schools to keep their kids safe while they were at work. It was the labor market. "Parents *would* play a much more active role in their kids' education if the labor market became more flexible. I think parents want to be more involved. They want to provide the kind of expertise they have, but it's not the way their own jobs are set up."

Many families did not have the option of working remotely. Suddenly the term "front-line worker" took on a much broader definition. In addition to the health care workers and first responders, it soon became clear that a host of other workers—often working at minimum wage—were also essential to any kind of smoothly functioning society.

Many of these "new front-line" workers did not have paid leave. Most low-wage workers—80 percent, according to CAP's estimate—had no paid vacation time, and nearly half (43 percent) had no paid sick leave.

"School closures had a substantial effect on working mothers' ability to fulfill work obligations," a Kaiser Family Foundation survey found. When schools closed:

- Women were more likely than men to take time off work because of childcare problems. Four in ten low-income women (38 percent) said they took time off because of school or day care closures.
- Nearly half of all women (47 percent) who had to take time off because their child's school or day care closed ended up taking unpaid sick leave.
- Over two-thirds of working mothers (68 percent) who were low-income and nearly three in four (74 percent) of those who worked at part-time jobs were not paid when they had to take time off because their child's school or day care was closed due to the pandemic.

And so, in increasing numbers, women simply left the labor force. Nearly one in ten women (8 percent) reported quitting their job for reasons related to COVID.

Low-income women were three times more likely to have to leave a job than higher-income women, with 17 percent of low-income women quitting compared with 5 percent of higher-income women. Women with a high school degree or less (12 percent) were more likely to leave a job than women with a bachelor's degree (5 percent).

In other words, the situation for families was a lot like the situation for students. Disparities that existed prior to the pandemic were magnified. A larger share of women of color and those who are low-income had to quit their jobs, as well as take on additional caregiving.[14]

When it became clear that vaccines would soon be available, teachers strongly urged that they move to the head of the line. A December resolution of the National Education Association (NEA) said: "NEA believes that educators should receive priority access to COVID-19 vaccines because of the importance of safe, equitable, and effective in-person instruction and support;

and our members' role in delivering nutrition, instructional materials, and remote instruction to our students even when school buildings are closed."[15]

Many states responded quickly. An *Education Week* tracker noted that in the first week of January, five states (Hawaii, Michigan, New York, Utah, and Idaho) gave teachers vaccine priority. By the end of January, twelve states, Puerto Rico, and the District of Columbia had given teachers priority access.[16] Yet, as figure 4.1 will show, it was not until March that more than half of all schools were back in person.

The passage of the Coronavirus Response and Relief Supplemental Appropriations Act made another $53 billion available to schools (roughly four times the funding provided in the CARES Act). This new influx of funding, which was called ESSER II, allowed schools to continue purchasing computers and provide high-speed internet access. Schools were also encouraged to use the funding to support programs that would address learning loss, including tutoring and summer school or extended school year programs.

Additional funding came from the American Rescue Plan (ARP). These funds were also sometimes known as ARP ESSER, just to make the acronyms more complicated. Between March 2020 and March 2021, more than $189 million in federal funding was designated for K–12 COVID relief. The spending on technology earned solid marks from Andrew Ko. "In most cases—providing both devices and connectivity—things may not have been perfect, but public school leaders have done a terrific job."[17]

CHALLENGES FOR THE YOUNGEST LEARNERS

Clearly, for many students, virtual learning did not equate to in-person learning. Children who most needed personal contact with teachers paid the heaviest price. The youngest students, who had little or no exposure to in-person school, were even more disadvantaged.

The spring of 2020 had been a real challenge for Mary Robb Wilson. In order to get her kindergarten daughter logged on to the school and set up for her school day, Wilson said, "I had to sit my two-year-old in front of the TV. As a parent, you start to ask yourself about those tradeoffs—whether the juice was worth the squeeze."

With two other families, the Wilsons hired a preschool teacher to run a learning pod throughout the summer. That in-person, active learning gave children a chance to reconnect with the parts of school that they really enjoyed.

Then came the fall of 2020, which was "horrendously hard." In addition to the pandemic, two major wildfires raged through the Napa Valley. The family had to evacuate, "and we spent the first week of our daughter's first-grade year dialing into school from a hotel in Reno, Nevada."

Shortly after the new year, Wilson's daughter was able to return to her classroom. But even though she had started the pandemic "enamored with school," Wilson says that some of that love started to wear off as the year dragged on. Children spent less time in school. That meant less time for the special classes like science and art that she really loved. She was bored.

And while her daughter wasn't "struggling enough to require additional learning help, she also was not thriving." The teacher, dealing with students with a wide range of skills and abilities, was "somewhat limited in the bandwidth of what she was able to provide for extra support."

Even more concerning to the Wilsons was the fact that even the children who were in the classroom seemed to be spending a great deal of their class time on their tablets. The teacher had both in-person and virtual students, and managing that instruction was a real challenge.

The so-called "hybrid" teaching models, which asked one teacher to instruct both children in a classroom and others at home on their devices, proved to be perhaps the biggest challenge of the entire pandemic, according to many teachers. An article in *Chalkbeat* quoted teachers as saying that this practice was "an instructional nightmare," with teachers feeling as though they couldn't help either the in-person or their online students.[18]

Although Myralyn McCabe is an art teacher, she also worked with students on literacy skills. One of her young students was an English learner whose parents spoke only Spanish.

Somehow, the child's Zoom connection got stuck with a virtual background. The child was too young to be able to figure out how to take it off. McCabe tried to translate into Spanish so the parents could take the background down. Nothing worked. So when the literacy activity called for writing a letter on a white board and holding it up for her to see, the board was invisible.

NOT THE TRADITIONAL FIRST
DAY OF KINDERGARTEN

The decision of whether—and how—to send a child to school in the fall of 2020 was difficult for most parents. Should they take a chance that schools would really reopen? Should they start preparing for virtual learning? No one really knew what was best. And for the parents of the youngest kids, the decision was even more challenging because their kids might never have *been* in a school classroom.

That was the situation faced by Kwame B. and his wife in September 2020, as they helped their son adjust not only to kindergarten, but also to virtual school.

They set up a desk in the playroom and helped him learn how to log in. "The school provided a Chromebook and gave every child login information," Kwame said. "But he was obviously just learning how to read, so that really had only so much value. What it meant for us was that one of us had to get him logged in every day."

After getting him set up for the day, however, they weren't sure what their role as parents should be. "We didn't have any sense of if (or how) we should be engaged," Kwame said. "We were trying to figure out where the line was. Were we de facto teacher aides, making sure he was sitting down and paying attention? Or were we supposed to take a step back so the teacher could command the virtual room?"

It was a balancing act. Their five-year-old, like other children his same age, wasn't used to sitting still in a seat all day. It would have been an adjustment for him to get used to doing that in a school. But it was even more of a challenge "when he knew there were snacks downstairs and play equipment outside."

There were additional sensitivities involved. "This was his first foray into school proper and we are in an elementary school that is majority white. He was one of just a handful of nonwhite students in the class. We were keenly aware of his presence as a young black boy in a predominantly white space." That meant they never felt they had the option of just letting things ride.

Academically, they felt their son had arrived in kindergarten already meeting many of the learning goals for the year. While kindergarten children were supposed to learn to count to 30, their son arrived on Day One with the ability to count to 100. Similarly, the school's kindergarten goal was to have children learn their letters. He not only knew all the letters, but he also knew what sounds they made. "That meant he could build on those skills and make real progress even in what was honestly a less-than-ideal learning environment."

But as the family paid attention to what was going on in their son's kindergarten class, they were struck by how "the pandemic really laid bare the haves and the have nots. As it relates to learning and preparation, he came into it as one of the haves. And with the efforts of both what the teachers were doing at school and what we were doing at home, he was able to build a real momentum. But for us as a society, the pandemic has laid bare how fragile our societal structures are."

AN EFFORT TO GET SOME STUDENTS
BACK IN SCHOOL

As the school year continued and children remained out of their classrooms, evidence continued to mount that virtual learning was not meeting the needs of most students. In Virginia, Fairfax County Public Schools reported an 83 percent increase in the number of middle and high school students receiving an F in two or more classes. Schools that enrolled more low-income students stayed closed longer. By the fall of 2021, low-income students had lost more than a semester of learning. Harvard's Thomas Kane observed, "What happened in spring 2020 was like flipping off a switch on a vital piece of our social infrastructure. Where schools stayed closed longer, gaps widened; where schools reopened sooner, they didn't."[19]

States across the country saw the same pattern. By the time Governor Jay Inslee ordered the Washington schools to reopen in the spring of 2021, he noted that already that school year, 25 percent of all high school students hadn't received academic credit in at least one course, a huge jump from the year before. Students of color and those living in poverty were significantly less likely to be earning credit in all their classes.[20]

Some districts worked hard to bring children back to school for in-person learning at least some days each week. The Bedford, Massachusetts, school district instituted a hybrid learning model early in September of 2020. "I have never been so grateful," said Sarah Johnson.

Their daughter went to school on Monday and Thursday. Other students went on Tuesday and Friday, and everyone was remote on Wednesday. "That meant no student was at school for two consecutive days," she said. It seemed to limit the spread of the virus, since there were no COVID closures.

When students were at home, they signed on to their iPad and watched activity in the classroom. An assistant teacher facilitated the Zoom chat room for students who were online. Early in the pandemic, the community's Kids' Club opened up for students to do their remote learning. There were other students from Johnson's daughter's class, so they could sit together, albeit masked and socially distanced, and play outside when the weather allowed. When it was time to change classes, someone at the center would help students make that change.

On two other days, her daughter could be in her regular classroom. Again, students were masked and socially distant, but they could be with their teacher. "First grade is when you really learn to read," Johnson says. "It was important that her teacher could make regular in-person checks to see how she was progressing." In February, the schools returned to full-time, in-person learning.

In December, Fairfax County parents heard a rumor that the school system was going to bring back the children for in-person school four days a week. Using her son's IEP as the catalyst, Suzann Gallagher asked that he be included in the group that would come back first. The school principal denied her request and told her the decision was out of her hands.

"I had been patient," Suzann said. "But when I learned that the school system was prioritizing non-disabled kids (who were the children of school employees) over students with IEPs, "my patience came to a pretty quick end."

She filed a complaint with the state. After a state caseworker reached out to her and the school system, they were able to broker an agreement. Her son was readmitted in the first group of students brought back for in-person learning. They provided additional remediation to make up for the nearly one year he had been out of school.

"If I had not known how to work the system," she says, "my son would have continued to sit at home." She shared her experience with the parents of other students with disabilities so they could also advocate for their children. By April, all students in the system were back in classrooms.

STUDENTS BEGAN TO CHECK OUT

As 2021 began, both attendance and attentiveness remained an issue. Student absences increased by 60 percent for middle school students in January 2021 compared with the same month the year before. Absences doubled in that same time frame for students who were English learners or whose families lived in poverty. Nationwide, the students who most needed to be in school were not showing up.

Eventually, many of those virtual dropouts simply never came back to school. Total K–12 enrollment dropped by roughly 3 percent in 2020–2021 compared with the previous school year. That would represent a drop of roughly 1.5 million students, according to the National Center for Education Statistics (NCES).

There were reductions in enrollment across the United States, but some states experienced a greater decline. Twenty-nine states lost between 1 and 3 percent of their students year over year; Vermont, Mississippi, and Puerto Rico each saw declines of more than 5 percent.[21]

The Los Angeles Unified School District lost eleven thousand students from the previous year, dropping enrollment numbers below six hundred thousand students, the lowest point in three decades.[22] Statewide, California reported a drop of more than 2.6 percent, or more than one hundred sixty thousand students.

WHERE DID STUDENTS GO?

As with all education decisions, the reasons families enrolled their kids or not were varied. But there are a few key reasons why students did not come to school and where they went instead.

They Kept Preschoolers Out for an Additional Year

Enrollment data from across the country shows that the largest enrollment declines were in pre-K and kindergarten. According to the data from the National Center for Education Statistics, the combined number of preschool and kindergarten students decreased by 13 percent from the previous school year. The percentage of children ages three and four enrolled in school fell from 54 percent in 2019 to 40 percent in 2020, the first time since 1996 that fewer than half of the children in this age group were enrolled.[23] All told, the enrollment decline was the largest in more than twenty years.

Declines in kindergarten enrollment were not evenly distributed among the population. A *New York Times* investigation found that some cities lost many more students than the national average. In Philadelphia, kindergarten enrollment was down 28 percent. Jackson, Mississippi, had a 24 percent drop.[24]

And, of course, as with other pandemic-related consequences, the children who could least afford to miss school were often the ones who missed out. In neighborhoods below and just above the poverty line, where the average household income for a family of four was $35,000 or less, kindergarten enrollment losses were 28 percent larger than in the rest of the country.

There were larger declines in cities, and in schools that were all remote. For essential workers, many of whom were in low-paying jobs, finding somewhere safe for their children was essential. If school could not meet that need, they would keep their children in day care rather than enrolling them in kindergarten.[25]

They Shifted to Private or Charter Schools

Families who needed their children to be in school began to search for alternatives. Many looked at the private or charter schools that were open. And when in the spring of 2020 the Drewry family received the notice that schools would be closed for the remainder of the school year, "We just knew we had to start making a plan for the coming year."

That sense that they needed a different approach got stronger the longer remote learning continued. Their two older boys, then in fifth and third grade, had a very different reaction to virtual schooling. "Our fifth grader is an independent learner, and he liked the challenge of doing things on his own. Without much parental involvement, he sat in the office with my husband and could pretty much handle things on his own," she said.

But their third grader had a different response. "He spent his time with me, and he just needed a lot more parental involvement." Logging in for one class and then changing to a different platform for another class was a challenge. It was also hard at times to stay engaged with the learning activities the teachers presented.

"I saw for myself how hard the teachers were working, and they were doing an amazing job," Aimee says. "But had I not been sitting with my third grader, there is no way we would have navigated all those links."

They paid close attention to the district's announced plans for reopening in September. In July, FCPS notified parents that they would remain virtual, with no announced date for resuming in-person instruction. The Drewrys felt "defeated," Aimee said. "I knew that what we went through for the spring was not going to be good for our family. My husband and I had work we had to do. Our middle son was not doing as well in virtual school as he had in person." The family began looking for an alternative.

It came in an email from the small private school where the boys attended summer camp. "We're open," the message said. "We will be open in the fall."

"And we just jumped on it," Drewry said. "We thought it might just be for a year and then we would go back to public school. But we knew we needed in-person learning."

They went through the application process, the boys took some assessments, and then the family "raced around" getting uniforms and school supplies. When Aimee dropped them off at the school on the first day, "I cried tears of joy. They were so happy to be going back to school. And I knew they were in a place where they would be safe and be with friends and keep learning."

Enrollment statistics from the National Association of Independent Schools show that this family was not alone in making the move to a private school. Private schools reported a net enrollment growth of 1.7 percent over the two pandemic years.

Private preschool enrollment jumped even more. It grew by 21 percent in 2021–2022 and was up a net of 6 percent over two years.[26]

In Virginia, where the state department of education does not track private school enrollment, many private schools reported enrollment increases, with one Alexandria private school reporting a 35 percent enrollment increase in 2020 and 2021.[27]

They Homeschooled Their Children

Okay, it's fair to say that *every* parent was home schooling during at least part of 2020. But when the new school year started, some families decided that if their kids were going to school at home, then they would formally start to homeschool them. (At least that way they'd know if school would be in session every day.)

The US Census Bureau tracked the increase in home schooling between spring and fall of 2020. In April, about 5.4 percent of US households with school-age children reported that they were home schooling. By fall, that number had more than doubled, to 11.1 percent. The Census Bureau even added clarification to the question to be sure that households were reporting, as they said, "true home schooling rather than virtual learning through a public or private school."[28]

Chad and Gabriella Aldeman had struggled through Fairfax County's initial efforts at virtual learning with their kindergartener and their second grader. But the technology issues described in chapter 2 combined with a general "brittleness" of the system left both them and their kids wanting something different. "The logins were complicated. We were never quite sure which Zoom room they were supposed to be in for which class. And there simply wasn't very much learning time in any given day," Chad said. When the county offered parents the option to sign up for hybrid learning during the 2020–2021 school year, "we signed up for it." But in August, Fairfax County was one of the large districts that walked back that option, announcing instead that the schools would provide only virtual learning, at least for the start of the school year. "So we decided to homeschool."

They went on the state website to find the grade-level learning standards for each child. They purchased workbooks to help their kids tackle those standards. Gabriella developed lesson plans for science and social studies. Chad took over physical education. They found online apps like Khan Academy that would focus on other skills their kids needed. "Basically, we just cobbled things together," Chad recalled.

They understood how fortunate they were to have the job flexibility that allowed them both to work from home. They had the income to purchase things like online subscriptions for learning activities. "And still it was hard."

Home schooling became more popular with diverse parents. Rates for Black students nearly quintupled, rising from 3.3 percent to 16.1 percent. Hispanic families also nearly doubled their rate of home schooling, from 6.2 percent to 12.1 percent, according to the Census Bureau. Alaska (with an increase of 17.9 percent), Florida (13.1 percent), and Vermont (12.8 percent) were the states showing the largest jumps. But every state in the union showed an increase in the numbers of home schoolers.

They Created Pandemic Pods

One of the most popular, or at least most publicized, approaches to home schooling was the creation of "pandemic pods." These "microschools" were ad hoc alternatives that allowed parents to juggle the demands of their full-time work, parenting, and an online schooling program that frequently involved heavy parental participation.

Parents were motivated to join or create pods for several reasons. First, many parents wanted their children to have a chance to be with other kids. When the Center for Reinventing Public Education (CRPE) studied these learning pods, they found that just giving children a chance to be with other kids was a huge incentive. Without that contact, parents said their children were lonely and missed friends. That led to anxiety and stress and sometimes to more serious issues.

Equally important to many parents was the need to continue their own work. Even for parents who were no longer required to go into the office, there were still work responsibilities that had to be met. One parent told the researchers, that her child had started remote learning at home, but supervising her was in constant conflict with her professional responsibilities. She said that soon reached "a point where I was like, 'I can't do this and hold a job.'" So she formed a pod instead.[29]

Although parents had some concerns about learning loss, particularly after a largely miserable spring of virtual learning, that was not the main reason they set up learning pods, according to Jennifer Poon, a Fellow at the Center for Innovation in Education and one of the authors of the study. "Parents know that school is . . . a place where students learn content but also learn how to get along with others," she said. "They found themselves saying, 'Let my kid just not be alone.'"

Typically, a small group of families would come together so their children could do in-person schooling under the supervision of a parent or a tutor. But the exact organization of the pods, and the instructional approaches they used, were as varied as the families who set them up.

Frequently families first met online (Facebook had a national Pandemic Pod page as well as many city-specific pages to bring interested families together). Some pods were intentional about recruiting people who shared basic values—everything from mask wearing to whether students needed to complete an assignment before they could go play. Pods that didn't have those conversations in the beginning tended to have to face them later when problems arose.

While those pressures tended to create fairly homogenous groups of students, some families reported that their pod created a safe space for their child, according to Poon. "Pods that were designed especially for Black families, for example, could shelter students from the marginalizing feelings they sometimes felt in schools."

Most pods hired an adult to supervise student learning. The more affluent the families in the pod, the more likely they were to hire a certified teacher. The national average cost for hiring a pod instructor was $306 per week, according to CRPE.[30] For an individual family, that cost over nine months would nearly equal the average cost of a private school ($11,000).

In more than half the pods included in the CRPE study, parents ended up hiring teachers to direct the learning. "Parents really did want a place where their children could keep learning," Poon said. "It was not just about child care."

A Learning Pod in Action

Nicole Christensen's decision not to struggle with virtual learning for her kindergarten daughter after the Boulder Valley School District closed its schools was described in chapter 2. She said that by May of 2020, she already figured schools were unlikely to reopen in the fall. "I run a small fitness business and I was keeping track of the spread of the virus," she said. "Things did not seem to be moving in the right direction to allow schools to reopen."

In addition, she said, "I knew I was going to have to travel for work. The idea of managing all of that *and* supervising two kids' daily virtual learning just seemed like an impossibility."

She began reaching out to friends to see whether they might set up some sort of learning pod. Eventually, four families, with eight children ranging from kindergarten through third grade, agreed that they were willing to give the idea a try. One family volunteered their walk-out downstairs as the classroom. Easy access to the outdoors made it possible for the school to incorporate the kind of physical activities the families valued.

Several of the families had experience with the Montessori approach to education. The emphasis on building responsibility and independence was appealing to everyone.

Teacher Shelley Reynolds, a Montessori-trained educator, had been teaching in a school she reached via a long drive over mountain roads. When Nicole first broached the idea of working with eight children in a pod, she was happy to work closer to home.

Colorado's regulations governing home schooling meant that the school would need to be set up as a parent co-op and that parents would need to be onsite every day. Reynolds did the research and set up a program that complied with the state's requirements.

But as for teaching a multi-age group of students? "I just teach—I teach kids in big groups, I teach kids in small groups. I teach preschoolers and I teach adults. I was not worried about handling a group of diverse learners. It wasn't a personal challenge; it was a personal opportunity," she said.

Besides, Reynolds was confident that "a one-room-schoolhouse approach would work." A friend's mother had recently retired from teaching in a one-room K–8 school in rural Minnesota, so Reynolds talked with her. "We had the best conversations when I would just ask, 'How did you do this? How did you do that?'"

The Roots Co-op, as it was known, followed an eight-week-on, two-week-off schedule. While some pods had strictly enforced quarantine rules, this one was not rigid. Nonetheless, "for most of our kids, these were the only other children they saw."

Christensen drew up a parent handbook that laid out expectations for each family. Because parents would be in the classroom every day, Reynolds made sure they understood the need for confidentiality about anything they learned about other children.

While some pod teachers had to take on the responsibility of ensuring that they were paid, that was not the case at the Roots Co-op. As a small business owner, Nicole and another parent had negotiated a contract that provided a guaranteed salary and benefits, including health care. "We wanted to pay Shelley more than she had been earning," she said. Parents knew their financial responsibilities before they signed on.

True to the Montessori approach, Reynolds drew up a learning plan for every student every day. There were times when students worked on specific assignments. "I knew that they would eventually be going back to classrooms where they had to work on specific subjects at specific times, so we got them prepared for that," she said. There were math facts to learn. Reading lessons ranged from phonemic awareness for the younger students to finding the main idea for older children.

Sometimes, students had choices. Even so, Reynolds says, she was not afraid to guide their choices. "I would tell them that I noticed when they were reading, sometimes there were sight words that would trip them up. I'd ask them to spend some time during their reading free-choice time working on those sight words."

The Roots Co-op was so successful that it continued for a second year, even after the schools reopened. But as children got older, parents were interested in bringing them back to their public school.

Older Students Dropped Out

In the years before the pandemic, the dropout rate in the United States had shown a steady decline. US Department of Education statistics showed the dropout rate falling from roughly 10 percent in 2006 to 5 percent in 2018.

Even in 2020, as schools waived graduation requirements, the dropout rate continued downward.

But the Class of 2021 faced different challenges. Online learning continued for many students. Teens got jobs to help their families financially. Or they spent their days watching younger siblings so their parents could work.

Students stopped coming to class, whether in person or online. Many states reported increases in absenteeism. Students felt disengaged—there were no proms to look forward to, and in many cases no athletics to give students a reason to be in school.

Full numbers will not be available until 2023. But it appears that after more than a decade of improving graduation rates, the pandemic will have reversed that trend. *Chalkbeat* collected graduation rates from twenty-six states (the others are still being calculated). The results showed declines in most of those states. "The coronavirus may have ended nearly two decades of nationwide progress toward getting more students diplomas," the report concluded.

Even the students who graduated from high school seemed less likely to enroll in postsecondary education. The National Student Clearinghouse reported a 13 percent decline in freshman enrollment since 2019, including a 32 percent decline for African American students in public two-year colleges and a 20 percent decline for Latinx students.[31]

Those numbers are particularly troubling given the changing requirements of the workforce that these high school graduates would enter. Today, 80 percent of well-paying jobs require postsecondary education and 56 percent require a bachelor's degree or higher. Additionally, those with postsecondary education are far less vulnerable to economic downturns. During the Great Recession, for example, the unemployment rate for people with a bachelor's degree or higher never exceeded 5 percent. During the COVID-recession, the unemployment rate for people with a bachelor's degree never went above 8.4 percent, whereas the unemployment rate for people with a high school degree but no college reached 17.6 percent.[32]

One of the continuing impacts of the pandemic, then, will be fewer high school graduates using education as a way to prepare for a higher-wage job. While some students may enroll in community college or a four-year college later in their lives, many more may be stuck in low-wage, low-skill jobs for the rest of their lives.

GETTING STUDENTS ONLINE

Most problems facing education can't really be solved just by spending more money. But technology is one place where money can actually lead to positive results. As discussed earlier in this chapter, roughly $190 billion in new

K–12 funding allowed for major technology investments. In the second half of 2020, school districts made real headway in ensuring that students had computers or tablets and some way to access the internet.

It wasn't always easy. Supply-chain issues involving devices that included many parts manufactured in China made the job even harder. At one point there were simply no Chrome books available for purchase anywhere in the United States.

The inequities that define schooling in the COVID era also cropped up here. In more affluent districts, many students owned personal computers so the district needed to make fewer purchases in order to ensure all students could go online. But in districts that served primarily low-income students, many fewer had access to devices at home. And those districts had less money to purchase the devices.

"As with many other issues in education, student connectivity at home was correlated to family income," said Reg Leichty, a founding partner of Foresight Law + Policy. "But geography also had an impact. Low-income kids were less connected at home. Rural students were less connected at home. And in the rural areas, everything was disproportionately worse for children of color."

That was the experience of Myralyn McCabe's students in Flagstaff, Arizona, and the nearby Navajo Reservation had to cope. There was often no internet available in the very rural areas where they lived. Or if it was available, it was too expensive.

Instead, in 2020, families sat in school parking lots so students could download their school assignments. Because so many kids lacked the technology for virtual learning, teachers posted assignments to their individual website. It was not until the next school year that the district was able to provide enough devices and internet hot spots, as well as Zoom technology, to get every student online.

But help, in the form of significant federal funding, made it possible for schools to close those gaps. The CARES Act had provided the first tranche of funding that could be used to purchase technology to support virtual learning. ESSER I and ESSER II made significantly more money available to address the costs associated with COVID.

Roughly 40 percent of districts announced they would allocate at least some of the ESSER funds to technology purchases. However, these expenditures had to compete with making up for lost learning time and addressing students' social and emotional needs.[33] But ESSER funding, followed by two more massive infusions of federal aid to education, did mean that for most districts, it was eventually possible to provide a device and connectivity to every student.

"For many districts," Leichty said, "these federal investments made it possible to take their ten-year technology plans and turn them into one-year plans. As a result, there are now a lot more devices in schools."

Federal funding was available to address the connectivity gap. Additional broadband funding, for example, was included in the American Rescue Plan Act (ARP). Billions of dollars from ARP could be applied to building out infrastructure, reducing prices to consumers, and funding the development of digital skills for more Americans.

States also provided additional funding. By fall 2021, forty-four states had created their own state-funded grant programs to cover costs of deploying high-speed internet in areas where it would otherwise not be economically feasible.[34]

State programs typically focused on projects that would increase service and speed and expand the locations where high-speed internet could be available. Most of these grant programs were "technology neutral"—in other words, they would fund both connecting via a wire (as in broadband) or via a cellular connection (such as 5G).

Leichty commends both the federal funding plans and many state plans for a focus on equity. "The infrastructure bill committed $65 billion for broadband access. One of the requirements of that funding was to target unserved or underserved communities." In addition, many states also required or encouraged any program funded by state grants to prioritize affordability and access for low-income communities.

After districts found enough devices, they still had to figure out how to get them into the hands of students. At least one district—the Los Angeles Unified School District—took lessons they had learned from the school lunch program (described in chapter 2) as they worked to get computers into students' hands.

Andrew Ko, a former member of the Virginia State Board of Education, consulted with the Los Angeles Unified School District as they grappled with the problem. "The sheer logistics of moving more than thirty thousand devices into kids' hands was pretty daunting," Ko recalled.

In Los Angeles, school lunch programs had deployed Grab and Go lunch distribution sites throughout the district. Ko says the school district initially thought they could use those sites to hand out computers. But public health officials denied the request, fearing that the time required for parents to sign the forms acknowledging they had the devices would simply be too long and would present too much of a danger of spreading COVID.

Although Ko worked for Amazon Web Services, he knew the company also had logistics programs developed to deliver goods during natural disasters. Ko negotiated an agreement with Amazon.com drivers to allow them to deliver the devices to the homes of each student.

First, of course, the district wanted to know the home address of each student—always a challenge in a large district with many transient families. A first delivery of a school lunch confirmed that the student actually lived at the address and that there was someone there to sign for the package. The next day, the district followed up by delivering the devices. "And that is how LA Unified delivered more than thirty thousand devices across the seven hundred square miles within the district's boundaries," Ko says.

That kind of program, drawing on the expertise of corporate partners with experience in logistics, was replicated across the country. "In essence, we Door Dashed tens of thousands of computers to students," Ko says.

CHAPTER 4

THE PANDEMIC'S LINGERING ACADEMIC IMPACT

The COVID-19 pandemic has exacerbated a lot of problems facing public schools—but it didn't create most of them. Most of the inequities existed long before the pandemic. The only difference is who was affected and who was paying attention.

—Meghan Mangrum, education reporter

In 1972, Chinese premier Zhou Enlai was asked what he thought about the impact of the French Revolution (which took place in 1789). His response: "Too early to say."

That may be the best way for all of us to think about the impact of the pandemic closings of 2020–2021. For students, teachers, and families, the effects of school closures were still being felt long after students were back in school buildings. It may be years before we sort out what happened and how school closures affected students.

Students experienced both academic losses and mental health stresses. Their parents were more likely to experience burnout. The Yale School of Medicine published an article in May arguing that "The impact of schools closing their doors for a third of a calendar year due to the COVID-19 pandemic will be devastating for students' potential."[1]

The first day of any new school year is always a festive occasion. But the 2021–22 school year was anything but normal. Students returned to schools that had changed in significant ways, with everything from staff shortages to significant drops in student enrollment. Students are still coping with the mental health challenges they faced during school closure. They have arrived in classrooms unprepared to do the work that teachers would ordinarily expect them to be able to do. Families are often still struggling with financial losses.

SCHOOL ITSELF CHANGED

Enrollment was down. Many of the students who left public schools during virtual learning did not return. Many first graders arrived in school never having set foot in a classroom. Many second graders, having missed part of kindergarten and all of first grade, had not mastered basic literacy or numeracy skills.

More than two hundred thirty thousand students had lost parents and caregivers to COVID.[2] Over fifty million households with children had lost income because of COVID. Child abuse cases had spiked.

Staff shortages—from bus drivers to substitute teachers—have made it harder for schools to provide basic services. The Associated Press reported that 80 percent of school districts were having trouble hiring bus drivers. The mayor of Chicago even reached out to ride sharing companies Uber and Lyft to help get kids to school after bus drivers quit over a mask mandate.[3] In the Chesterfield, Virginia, school district, a top FBI official came out of retirement to drive a school bus, which was, he said, just a continuation of his commitment to public service.[4]

One Delaware district offered to pay parents $700 if they would be responsible for getting their kids back and forth to school. Pittsburgh delayed the start of classes in hopes of having enough drivers on the first day. The district also expanded the boundaries for students who would have to walk to their school building to one and a half miles for elementary students and two miles for secondary students.[5]

School cafeteria workers, custodial workers, and office personnel were similarly in short supply. Substitute teachers were scarce.

The National Center for Education Statistics reported that nearly half (44 percent) of school districts had at least one vacancy for a full- or part-time teacher. Of those, 61 percent cited the COVID-19 pandemic as a cause of the increased vacancies. And the leading cause of vacancies was resignation, not retirement.[6]

In a December 20, 2021, "Dear Colleague" letter to school superintendents, US Secretary of Education Michael Corona laid out the challenge:

> Preexisting teacher shortages in critical areas such as special education; bilingual education; science, technology, engineering, and math; and career and technical education have been further exacerbated by COVID-19—directly impeding student access to educational opportunity. According to a recent Ed Week Research Center survey, one in four district leaders and principals are reporting severe staffing shortages.[7]

He suggested using ARP funding to help address the shortages. Among his possible solutions were temporary increases in teacher salaries and hiring more substitute teachers.

Given these changes, it is hard to see how schools could get back to anything like a "normal" school year. In fact, experience from other extended school closures suggests that the effects of the COVID closures will last much longer than anyone ever expected.

When an earthquake closed schools in Pakistan in 2005, the impact of those school closures extended for years. After students were able to return to school, test scores showed learning losses that were greater than the time they had missed out on school. (Students who missed a year of school experienced learning losses of greater than one year.) The learning losses were concentrated in families with less education, which meant that the natural disaster increased inequality. And the test score losses grew over time, even after children were back in school.[8]

In citing the study, Georgetown University's Chad Aldeman, a Fairfax County parent whose story is told in Chapter 3 noted, "Distance learning efforts overall went poorly, amplified inequities, and districts are poised to cut learning time again this year. . . . If nothing changes about this trajectory, we should be prepared for outcomes similar to those Pakistan experienced: Large and inequitable learning losses will hit the COVID generation of students, and those effects will carry on into the future, hurting the children directly and society indirectly down the road."[9]

In the United States, surveys showed that parents clearly saw evidence of learning loss—and worried about it. In October 2021, NPR, the Robert Wood Johnson Foundation, and Harvard T. H. Chan School of Public Health found that 69 percent of parents were concerned that their children had missed learning during remote schooling, and the available evidence suggests that those concerns are justified. Of those, 36 percent said they were "very concerned" about learning loss.[10]

Those parents were not looking for things to bounce back quickly. When asked to think about the upcoming school year, 70 percent of parents in households where children fell behind last year said they believed it would be difficult for their children to catch up on the learning loss. Of those, 14 percent said they thought it would be "very hard" for their children to catch up.

Some children will catch up, although it may be challenging. For others, it will be years, if ever, before they regain the learning they lost. Particularly for students with disabilities, the year of lost learning will, in fact, be a year of lost learning. Chapter 7 includes several stories of students whose learning may never return to where it was before the pandemic.

THE REALITY OF LEARNING LOSSES

From the earliest days of the pandemic, experts predicted that students would suffer significant learning losses. They were right.

"The learning losses have been significant thus far," said Dan Goldhaber, an education researcher at the American Institutes for Research. He acknowledged being perplexed by the tendency to avoid talking about the learning losses, even going to the extent of changing the nomenclature and talking about unfinished learning. "I don't so much care about the nomenclature," he said. "But I think a change in student achievement is a measurable phenomenon. We are measuring it. It is there."

A study by Harvard University's Center for Education Policy Research used scores on the MAP test to track student learning between 2019 and 2021. On average, students who attended in-person school for nearly all of 2020-21 lost about 20 percent worth of a typical school year's math learning between 2019 and 2021.

Students who stayed home for most of 2020-21 fared much worse. On average, they lost the equivalent of about 50 percent of a typical school year's math learning between 2019 and 2021. As Matt Chingos from the Urban Institute puts it: "Students learned less if their school was remote than they would have in person."[11]

Who were those students who spent the most time out of school? They were students in low-income districts. First, many of these districts are in cities, with active teacher unions and elected officials who were reluctant to send students back to in-person learning. And as the previous chapters have shown, low-income students were least likely to have access to devices and the high-speed internet they would need to be successful.

The impact of all of this will be long-lasting. "This will probably be the largest increase in educational inequity in a generation," Thomas Kane, an author of the Harvard study, told the *New York Times*.[12]

We do have at least one historical model in the United States that can provide some insight into the lingering effects of school closures: Hurricane Katrina. The two situations are not identical, but there are some lessons to be learned. Paul Hill from the Center for Reinventing Public Education talked with New Orleans educators, to gain their perspectives on what happened to students after schools closed.

- When students returned to their schools, they were on average more than two years below grade level, some much more. Losses were most dramatic in mathematics.

• The degree of learning loss couldn't be predicted by family income, prior school, student age, or pre-Katrina grade level.
• It often took multiple years of individualized attention to resolve the largest learning losses.[13]

As one New Orleans educator reflected, "A big trauma like Katrina can have effects for decades. Learning losses don't just disappear with one course or in one academic year. For schools, the need to keep track of where every child is, and to work constantly on helping everyone move along, is permanent, not short-term."[14]

Even in the first year after schools reopened, it was possible to determine that all three of these outcomes were also showing up in the students who came to be known as "Generation C" (for COVID). Data from the first year after students returned to the classroom seems to bear out the Katrina experience. By any measure, the COVID school closures had a dramatic impact on students' learning. There has been significant learning loss. It appears to be widespread, although students of color and students from low-income families faced more severe losses. And educators recognize that it will be many years before students entirely catch up.

The research organization NWEA tracked student learning throughout the pandemic. After schools had returned to in-person instruction, they measured how much progress students had made between the start of school in 2019 and in 2021. NWEA then compared that growth to what might have been expected in a pre-pandemic world. (In other words, what if students had spent the 2020–2021 school year learning in school instead of online?)

The results were both predictable and devastating. In both reading and math, student learning gains fell below expectations. The declines in fall 2021 achievement relative to fall 2019 ranged from 3 to 7 percentile points in reading and 9 to 11 percentile points in math.[15]

Similar findings came from the nationally administered test known as the i-Ready. Again, researchers found significant declines, especially among the youngest students and particularly in math.

For example, in third grade, 38 percent of students were below grade level in reading, compared with 31 percent historically. In math, 39 percent of students were below grade level, vs. 29 percent historically.[16] Students who need direct instruction and support from a teacher the most—low-income students, English learners, students with disabilities, and Black and Brown students—are likely to have experienced the most dramatic losses. But all students are expected to have some learning loss, with math losses more dramatic than losses in reading.

Education Week reporters Stephen Sawchuk and Sarah D. Sparks spoke with researchers about the difference. They offered three possible explanations:

- Unlike reading, math is almost always formally learned at school. Parents typically feel less prepared to help their children with math.
- Many students experience math anxiety. Stress and trauma (such as, say, a pandemic) can worsen math anxiety. In a vicious cycle, the math anxiety can in turn make students' other in-class stress even worse.
- It can be more challenging for teachers to engage in effective math instructional practices via remote platforms.[17]

Teaching math online is different from teaching math in a classroom. Even pre-COVID, many elementary teachers lacked both content and pedagogical knowledge for teaching mathematics. Many undergraduate elementary teacher preparation programs do not cover critical math topics including numbers and operations, algebra, and geometry. (And yes, all those are now taught in elementary school math.)[18]

When students start to fall behind in math, it is simply harder to catch up. As Sal Kahn, founder of the Kahn Academy, observed, "Concepts build on one another. Algebra requires arithmetic. Trigonometry flows from geometry. Calculus and physics call for all of the above. A shaky understanding early on will lead to complete bewilderment later."[19]

Conversations with parents confirm this research. Parents had a harder time helping children with math while they were at home. For Elena Guarinello and Jessica Latterman, helping their daughter with math at home was certainly a tougher go than English-language arts. "They teach them math in a whole other way from the way we learned," Elena said. "In fact, it's probably better than how we were taught math. But that meant that even when I knew how to get the answer to the problem, I couldn't really help her solve it the way the school wanted her to."

In addition, the language used in her daughter's math textbooks was a barrier. "A lot of the instructions seemed to be written in jargon. Finally, I just stopped trying to help."

Even more troubling, the data show that declines in student achievement increased learning gaps. Lower achievers showed lower normative growth between fall 2019 and fall 2021 compared to higher achievers in reading and math. Students who started out behind fell further behind.[20]

There had initially been some optimism about reading scores during the pandemic. But when researchers took a closer look at the youngest readers, that optimism declined. In particular, children whose critical first-grade year was spent online are more likely to struggle with foundational reading skills. These early years are where students build the skills they need for continued school success.

Stanford University researchers focused on literacy development in the earliest grades. They looked at oral reading fluency—the ability to read

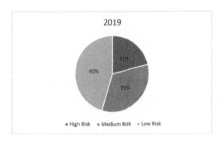
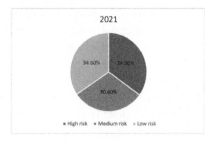

Figure 4.1. Virginia primary students at serious risk of reading difficulties

aloud quickly and with accuracy. It found that fluency largely stopped in 2020 when schools closed so abruptly. While students regained some fluency when they returned to in-person learning, it was not enough to make up for the initial learning loss.[21] The youngest students, those in second and third grade, experienced the greatest losses; the study estimates their fluency was roughly 30 percent behind where it would have been had the pandemic not closed schools.

Those results were similar to other studies. In Virginia, researchers at the University of Virginia found that the percentage of students in grades K–2 designated as at "high risk" for reading difficulties jumped by 66 percent in two years—from 21 percent in 2019 to 35 percent in 2021. Numbers were even higher for English learners, students with disabilities, and Black and Latino students. Figure 4.1 shows the dramatic increase.[22] Clearly, many students did not get the instruction they needed in literacy or in math during the pandemic. For the youngest learners, it may be especially challenging to catch up.

Elementary teachers often say that students learn to read first, and then they can read to learn. Students who do not learn to read proficiently by third grade struggle to "read to learn" thereafter and are four times less likely to graduate high school.[23] In these grades (typically grades three to five), students who do not master concepts like fractions and whole-number division will struggle even more in upper-level math classes. They are also less likely to graduate from high school on time.[24]

But the story on *which* students were *how far* behind was another reflection of the inequities of the pandemic. Students in majority Black schools had lost an additional five months of learning during the pandemic. Since they went into the extended school closures nine months behind expected performance, that meant that these students were now more than a full year behind.[25]

NWEA's MAP Growth assessment showed that students in more economically disadvantaged schools were the most affected by the pandemic. This unequal impact is particularly evident in the elementary grades, where the declines for students in high-poverty schools were noticeably larger than the declines for students in low-poverty schools.[26]

In short, COVID took a bad situation—the gap between middle-class white students and low-income students or students of color—and made it worse.

A K-SHAPED RECOVERY

Researchers began to see the similarities between the economic recovery from COVID and the educational recovery. Instead of a V-shaped recovery, they are now seeing a K-shaped recovery. Harvard economist Raj Chetty and colleagues at Opportunity Insights described how the COVID recession did not affect all Americans equally.

In the economy, affluent Americans recovered much more rapidly than what is usual in a typical recession. When COVID hit, high-income households cut back on their spending because of health concerns rather than because they had lost income. Most of these families were able to work at home and continued their regular earnings. But any spending that required an in-person interaction (restaurants, gyms, nail salons) and thus might expose them to COVID, were areas where these affluent families simply stopped spending.

Low-income workers, however, many of whom provided the services that affluent customers were now forgoing, lost their jobs. They were more likely to be quarantined and to have a family member infected with COVID. Their jobs did not come back rapidly. As a result, the economic recession was K-shaped. Affluent families recovered quickly. Lower-income families continued to see declines.[27]

The parallels to education are clear. For the kids whose parents enrolled them in webinars and online classes, who hired tutors and created learning pods, there probably will be a relatively limited time when they experience the negative consequences of school closure. And yet even for those families, pandemic school closures took a toll.

But for low-income families, those problems were multiplied. Early in the pandemic, their only internet-ready device was often a smart phone. Their child's only connection to the internet often came at school. As a result, when virtual school officially "opened up," these students were too often not there. And when in-person learning began, they were farther behind than before.

Myralyn McCabe has seen that in her school, which enrolls low-income students from the city of Flagstaff as well as from the nearby Navajo Reservation. Nearly all of them are behind; some are "so far behind I can't see how they will be able to do the work in the grade they now attend," she said. By far, the kids who have struggled the most are those whose families were overwhelmed by COVID. The virus swept through the reservation, and many families dealt with sick family members. Lost jobs and shortened work hours hurt family incomes.

All that meant that even when teachers tried to reach out to provide support, some families just couldn't take action. They couldn't drive the hour or more from their home to the school to pick up learning kits. They couldn't troubleshoot if there were internet problems because the kids probably knew more about technology than anyone in the family. And these students, the neediest in her school, will be dealing with the impact of COVID for the longest time.

"We already had this deep inequality in American education," said John Friedman, a Brown University professor of economics in an interview with *The 74*. "The pandemic has taken children and set them even further back. Without some really dedicated effort to get these students caught up, what we've seen from broader data is that the types of educational gaps that arise in childhood can persist, they create lower college enrollment rates, lower college graduation rates, students earn less when they get out in the labor market. These things can have really large effects down the line."[28]

MISSING CONTENT

In some cases, students at the start of 2021–2022 lacked the foundational content and knowledge from the previous year. Shelley Reynolds, who combined teaching in a pandemic pod with tutoring students in the local public school, says about the students who spent a virtual year, "They've lost a lot. Even after just four months of online learning, we had to really work hard together so they could close the gaps. Students really struggled, especially elementary kids."

One of Reynolds's teacher friends reported that her entire class of fourth graders arrived in class in the fall of 2021 not knowing how to multiply. It's a big part of the third-grade math curriculum in most places. But somehow, the students just hadn't learned it. Because math, more than any other subject, builds on what students have already learned, kids who don't know how to multiply will also struggle with fractions, ratios, and ultimately with algebra and other higher math classes.

That does not mean students can't learn multiplication. It likely does mean that they will not be able to learn everything that fourth-grade math typically covers. And besides putting them behind where they would have been, it can also affect their entire approach to learning.

That was the case for one of the families interviewed in this book. After their child had been back in school for about three months, the teacher asked them to write a five-paragraph essay. Now, there's nothing particularly hard about a five-paragraph essay, but it is formula writing, and it is one of those things that works only if students know the formula.

This child didn't. During the previous COVID year, the teacher just couldn't cover all the content that she usually would, and five-paragraph essays simply weren't taught that year.

As a result, the child got frustrated and upset. It wasn't just "I can't write this essay." It became, "I can't write." And it wasn't just "I'm not doing well in this grade," it was "I'm not good in school."

Again, the essay format is something the child could learn (and eventually did). But coming after a year of frustration and isolation that grew out of learning at home, it was just one more setback.

COPING CHALLENGES

In many rural districts, wild fires have become a major cause of school closure. In California before the pandemic, wildfires accounted for two-thirds of all school closures. But the combination of pandemic-related closures and wildfires wreaked a special havoc on the Wilson family in Napa Valley. For them, a return to school after the COVID closures was delayed still further by two raging wildfires that forced them to evacuate.

Eventually the fires were put out. But even after their daughter returned to her classroom, it didn't take long for the Wilsons to see that she was less and less excited about going to school. They were also starting to worry about the instruction their daughter was missing. So were many other parents. One poll taken in April of 2020 found that 69 percent of parents were worked that "my child is missing instruction time," and 46 percent were *very* worried.[29]

The youngest children often faced the biggest challenges. Learning to read often requires hands-on activities such as tracing letters. Kids who were at home couldn't always do those things. Parents of young children interviewed for this book noted that their children had much more trouble writing than their older children had at the same age.

For some of the foundational reading skills—things like hearing specific vowel sounds—"it really helps if children can see how the teacher's face is moving. It helps if the teacher can see how the child is moving her mouth.

That couldn't happen in school with masks, and so it was really almost better for kids to learn those skills virtually because they could take their masks off," Wilson said.

As she and her husband talked about the upcoming school year, they came to a hard realization: if they wanted a different outcome for their child, they were going to have to make a big shift. "It was just too early for our child to lose that sense of wonder and love for learning."

So they began to search for a school that they thought would be a better fit. They found one, a charter school that taught students for most of the day in an outdoor setting and that focused on using the inquiry method.

There was, however, a real issue. The school was in Wisconsin.

They flew to Milwaukee and toured the school. It seemed like a great fit for their three kids. And one benefit of the pandemic was that Wilson's husband, a winemaker in Napa, had negotiated the ability to work remotely during the off-season.

So they moved halfway across the country and enrolled their two youngest children in the charter school. Their older daughter, on a waiting list for the charter, started second grade in her local public school.

The assessment that the school gave their daughter confirmed their suspicions that she had not made the academic progress expected of a first grader. The school provided the intensive, research-based tutoring that would help her catch up in reading and math—thirty minutes, three times a week in each subject.

Would the family have moved if there had been no pandemic? It's hard to say. Wildfires and climate change were leading to more evacuations, and the Wilsons could see those risks increasing in the future.

But it's clear that one of the impacts of school closures for the Wilsons—and many other families—was a rethinking of priorities. Most families did not move halfway across the country to enroll their children in a different school. But they nonetheless made the move to a different school.

On the other side of the country, Margaret and Tom Millar had finally decided that after a difficult year of virtual school, they could not start another school year with their son in their neighborhood elementary school. It was a particularly hard decision because they had chosen their house especially *because* of the neighborhood school. Two years earlier, before their oldest child started kindergarten, they sold their house and moved. "Our old house was pretty small for our family, so we always knew we were always going to move," she says. But finding the right public school for their two boys was a high priority.

She works in education policy, and she did her homework. Ultimately, they bought a home in McLean, Virginia, feeling confident that the Fairfax County Public Schools would be a good fit for them.

It was not. Their son's kindergarten teacher, with twenty-nine students in the class, was overwhelmed and admitted that in their interactions. For first grade, they decided to enroll him in the French Immersion program.

But as the school start date drew nearer, Millar wrote to the principal, saying, "I don't know that this is the right option for us. Online learning is going to be really hard—I don't think that doing it in French will work." The principal said, "It will work out."

It did not work out. Her six-year-old started school with two teachers, one of whom spoke only French to teach math and science. "The kids couldn't use the technology. It was unstable and glitched every day, except for the days it didn't work at all."

Teachers for special subjects either didn't show up or would ask students to use yet another technology. There were different apps for every single class. "Except for music, where we had two," she said.

That meant a parent had to sit with the first grader all day to help him navigate. "I have a master's degree in the art of teaching," Millar said, "but this was just impenetrable. And of course, a lot of it was in French."

It was not, Millar emphasizes, the teachers who were making things difficult. It was simply an unworkable situation.

Meanwhile, the family's younger child was heading back to in-person preschool. The first grader begged to be able to be with other kids again. "I promise I would wear a mask," he said. "I just want to go to school."

The final straw came on the day when they went to school to pick up new Chromebooks as a way of getting students back in the classroom. Margaret and her son walked up to the desk and were asked to identify themselves. Margaret responded with her son's first and last name. "No," she was told. "We don't need his name. We need his *number*." And so on a day when her son was already anxious about returning to school, "what we felt was that no one actually cared about his name," she says.

The family had been considering whether they would return to the public school system for their son's second grade year. That day was not the only reason they made the decision to enroll him in private school, she says. "But it is one of those experiences I could not get out of my head." In the end, the family decided reluctantly that they would not return to the public school the next year.

"We had *moved* because we really wanted to be part of a public school system," Millar said. "But it was the sum total of how much our son had started to dislike school, how lost he was feeling, and our sense as a family that we were totally abandoned by the school system. We just got to a point where we thought we needed to hit the reset button."

These two stories illustrate what happened in aftermath of the 2020–2021 school closures. Families looked for alternatives—schools where they could be assured that their children could attend school every day, for example, or schools where class sizes would be smaller.

STUDENTS WITH DISABILITIES

If virtual schooling was difficult for every student, for students with disabilities, the time spent out of school was often devastating. Students with disabilities, even more than their peers, need face-to-face instructional time. A June 2020 brief published by the Annenberg Institute for School Reform at Brown University noted the importance of additional in-person instructional time for students with disabilities, and found, "Students with disabilities are one of the student populations likely to have regressed the most during COVID-related distance learning."[30]

That has been the case for Carol and Tom Uecker, who have custody of their grandson. Carol describes him as a "highly anxious child. He has ADHD and is on the autism spectrum." He was in the eighth grade when the pandemic closed schools in Duluth, Minnesota, where he was enrolled.

Even before the pandemic, his school performance was uneven. If he liked and trusted the teacher, he worked hard and did well. If not, he struggled. When he made a mistake, he would run to stand by his locker rather than stay in class. And while he was anxious about mixing with other students, he also "wanted to do it."

His favorite class was orchestra. He developed a real bond with the orchestra teacher and worked hard in the class. The teacher was even able to persuade him to go on a field trip, something he had always been afraid to try because of his fear of new things and new places. The orchestra played in a competition, knowing that the winners would be invited to perform at Orchestra Hall in Minneapolis. They won, and the Ueckers' grandson was looking forward to the trip. The concert was, sadly, one of the first casualties of COVID.

Carol and Tom, a former math and special education teacher, sat with him during the early days of online schooling. Their grandson had his own computer and "he is more computer savvy than either of us," Carol says. He would get signed into the class, and he would listen, but he did not want to participate. He muted his microphone. He covered his camera. "Somehow," Carol said, "his teachers still knew he was there."

Ninth grade brought new classes, new teachers, and a whole new school— all difficult adjustments for a kid who did not react well to change. He didn't want Carol or Tom to sit with him while he was doing online school. He began exhibiting behaviors they had never seen: yelling, swearing, even striking out. They backed off.

As before, that led to uneven performance. In some classes, he would do well. But a conflict with a math teacher led to real problems. She had a rigid set of requirements for how students had to do their assignments because, as she expressed to the students, she didn't want anyone in her class to cheat. "Our grandson saw that as an accusation against him personally," Carol said. Things spiraled downward.

Fortunately, the special education teacher had a talk with the math teacher. Working with Carol and Tom, they changed their grandson's IEP so that he was taking the class on a pass/fail basis.

The high school orchestra teacher spent the year with the nearly impossible task of trying to conduct an orchestra over Zoom. Carol's grandson wouldn't play his instrument because it didn't sound "the way it's supposed to," he said. Still, although he and the teacher had never met in person, the instructor kept in touch and tried to find ways to help Carol's grandson listen to the music they were playing in class.

Finally students were allowed to go back to school. They were masked and there were no sports or clubs. "It was sort of like a ghostly place," their grandson reported. "Nobody talked."

But with help and support, he did complete the ninth grade successfully. Still, Carol says, she wonders about the other special education students who did not have parents and grandparents as advocates.

In one national survey of more than fourteen hundred parents of students with learning and thinking differences, nearly six in ten—an astoundingly high number—reported that their children are a year behind because of the pandemic and may never catch up. In addition, 44 percent of parents of children with learning and thinking differences say their child's legal right to access an equitable education has been *abandoned* since the move to remote learning (emphasis mine).[31]

Reflecting the same disparities seen throughout the pandemic, race and income also affected outcomes for students with disabilities. In schools with the largest number of low-income and nonwhite students, only about one in three (31 percent) provided access to alternative service arrangements. In schools with fewer low-income students and children of color, kids with disabilities were able to receive alternative support nearly half the time.

VIRTUAL LEARNING HELPED SOME STUDENTS

In the fall of 2020, the Richmond, Virginia, schools made a decision to offer fully virtual learning to all students. Kara Stup's sixth grade son, who has autism, needed an instructional assistant to be successful. The schools' offer of ten hours a week of in-person assistance was insufficient to meet his need for support in every class every day. And because of some of her son's health issues, Kara was also reluctant to invite another person into her home regularly.

Instead, she took on the task of acting as her son's instructional assistant. One benefit was that she finally could see firsthand "the things that caused him to struggle. If I hadn't been able to support him at home, I know he would have languished in class."

Sometimes, her observations provided an opportunity for teachers not only to change the assignment for her son but for every student in the class. In a science class, one note-taking activity involved asking students to type a great deal of information in a relatively short time. Stup saw that the speed of the activity was frustrating for her son, who couldn't process his thoughts (or move his fingers) fast enough. Because he has a severe reading disability, speed reading was problematic. "If it's not dyslexia, it's a lot like it," she says.

After the class, she asked the teacher to call her. "We met in a video call that afternoon and discussed the challenges of the activity," Stup said. The teacher listened and adjusted the entire activity for the whole class. The new format gave students some of the less-important notes prepopulated on a form. "In my opinion this was much better for the entire class and better focused on learning not typing or writing," she said.

In the second year after the pandemic, the Richmond schools reopened. But Kara and her son's pediatrician had concerns about his return to in-person learning. The pediatrician feared that her son might be more likely to develop a very serious inflammatory condition when exposed to the COVID-19 virus. So Kara asked the school system to authorize a second year of virtual learning. "Continued virtual learning was a need and not just a choice for our family for this school year," she said.

Virtual Virginia provided the instruction, and Kara says the format worked well for her son. No lesson was longer than thirty minutes. There were opportunities for breaks and a chance for him to work on his class assignments in shorter chunks. "My son works really well if he can listen and then apply what he has learned," she said. "The virtual platform worked very well for him."

Still, he has real issues with reading. When it was time for a review of his IEP, Kara was clear about what she wanted to include. In the sections that asked about the parents' concerns and the challenges the student was facing, "I wrote out exactly what I wanted the IEP to reflect. After two years of being at home, I was the only person who knew what those issues were."

SOCIAL AND EMOTIONAL ISSUES

As students returned to the classroom, teachers were overwhelmed by student behavior issues. "They went through the roof," said Dan Domenech of AASA. "These kids arrived back in school just so needy."

In October of 2021, the American Academy of Pediatrics (AAP), the American Academy of Child and Adolescent Psychiatry (AACAP), and the Children's Hospital Association (CHA) declared a National State of Emergency in Children's Mental Health.[32] In a news article about the declaration, reporter Christine Vestal wrote, "The grief, anxiety and depression children have experienced during the pandemic is welling over into classrooms and hallways, resulting in crying and disruptive behavior in many younger kids and increased violence and bullying among adolescents."[33]

According to the federal Centers for Disease Control and Prevention, emergency department visits for suspected suicide attempts among adolescents jumped 31 percent in 2020 compared with 2019. In January of 2021, emergency room visits for suspected suicide attempts among girls ages twelve to seventeen were up 51 percent over the year before.[34] In February and March of 2021, emergency department visits for suspected suicide attempts were also 51 percent higher among girls aged 12–17 than during the same period in 2019.

Counterintuitively, a decline in reported child abuse cases was a red flag. In the early days of the pandemic, the number of child protective services cases handled in the states dropped by around 10 percent. At first glance, this federally reported data on child abuse might initially have seemed like good news.

But that drop in numbers really masked the fact that because there was less contact between teachers and students, educators simply did not know if abuse was taking place. School personnel are usually what is known as "mandatory reporters" in most states. In other words, if they suspect child abuse or neglect, they are required to report it to authorities.

The Associated Press collected data on child abuse reporting from thirty-six states and found that reports of child abuse dropped by 59 percent in the months after schools moved to online learning. During the pandemic, there was less contact. Some students stopped attending school. Others would turn off their cameras so teachers couldn't see them.

The lower numbers simply meant greater potential for harm. "There has not all of the sudden been a cure for child abuse and neglect," said Amy Harfeld, with the Children's Advocacy Institute. "Children who are experiencing abuse or neglect at home are only coming to the attention of [Child Protective Services] much further down the road than they normally would."[35]

In March 2022, the Centers for Disease Control (CDC) released data about the "seismic impact" the pandemic had on teens during the pandemic. Data from the first half of 2021 revealed that teens experienced high levels of emotional distress. Nearly half (44.2 percent) said they had persistent feelings of sadness or hopelessness that kept them from participating in normal activities, and 9 percent said they had attempted suicide. Eating disorders that led to emergency room visits by teenage girls doubled during the pandemic.[36]

The CDC also found high rates of abuse, with 55.1 percent of teens saying they suffered emotional abuse from a parent or other adult in their house, including swearing at, insulting, or putting down the student. Physical abuse, defined as "hitting, beating, kicking, or physically hurting the student," was experienced by 11.3 percent of teens.[37]

"While the pandemic has affected all students, the experiences of disruption and adversity have not affected all students equally," the CDC report said. "Female students and those who identify as . . . LGBQ are experiencing disproportionate levels of poor mental health and suicide-related behaviors."

In addition, the report noted a rise in hunger among adolescents. Nearly one-third of Black students reported there was not enough food in their home.

Students weren't the only ones who experienced mental health issues during the pandemic. Parents who had spent more than a year struggling to combine their work responsibilities with being a parent, while also teaching long division, started to burn out. These parents saw the stress their children were facing, and it worried them.

A study in the *Journal of Family Issues* cited research showing that within one week of the federal social distancing guidelines being put into place, 15 percent of the parents in the survey reported that they had increased discipline of their child from the time when the pandemic began. Parents also reported deteriorating mental health, lower patience with their children, and heightened feelings of being overwhelmed by parenthood.[38]

"The stresses and pressures of being a parent combined with the demands of work have made life nearly impossible," one British parent told researchers in a McKenzie study of parents in the workplace. In that study, four in five employed parents said that they felt concerned about their child's mental health, and more than one-third rated this concern as extreme.

Chapter 3 outlined how parents used leave days, when they had them, to deal with school closures. But even though those parents had little time off, it was surprising that more than half (53 percent) also reported missing one or more days of work because of burnout.[39]

ENROLLMENT DECLINES AND
ABSENTEEISM CONTINUES

Students simply disappeared during COVID. The short version of the data on student enrollment and absenteeism: there were fewer students enrolled, and they came to school less often.

First, the number of students enrolled in schools continued to drop. Particularly in the nation's largest school systems, there were fewer students in classrooms. NPR surveyed six hundred districts in twenty-three states (data from the National Center for Education Statistics was not available as this book was completed). Their reporting included significant declines:

- New York City, which lost thirty-eight thousand in 2020–2021, lost another thirteen thousand in 2021–2022
- Los Angeles lost seventeen thousand students in 2020–2021 and another nine thousand in 2021–2022
- Chicago, which was down fourteen thousand in 2020–2021, lost another ten thousand students in 2021–2022.[40]

In Fairfax County, fall 2021 enrollment declined more than ten thousand students since fall of 2019, or a 5.4 percent difference between fall 2019 and fall 2021, according to the Virginia Department of Education. To put that into perspective, that is as many students as would be enrolled in a typical high school pyramid (one high school, one middle school, and five or six elementary schools). Fairfax County's student loss was the largest in Virginia, but the entire commonwealth showed a continued decline in enrollment of roughly 3.6 percent between 2019 and 2021.

Absenteeism continued a pattern that began in the earliest days after schooling went virtual. Student absences continued to rise.

In the spring of 2020, students often didn't have the technology that would allow them to sign on to a virtual class. But even after students received the technology, and then after schools reopened for in-person schooling, absenteeism continued. In March 2022 (two full years after schools first closed), the Los Angeles Unified School District (LAUSD) reported that nearly half (46 percent) of its students had not just been absent, but *chronically* absent. That designation means students had missed at least 9 percent of the academic year.

In a normal year, LAUSD already had high rates of student absenteeism. In the three years before the pandemic, the rate of chronic absenteeism had hovered around 19 percent. But in the 2021–2022 school year, the figure reached 46 percent.[41]

There are many reasons that chronic absenteeism jumped so dramatically. Lack of access to transportation, loss of parents and caregivers to COVID-19, and the economic upheaval faced by many families during the pandemic are all part of the problem. So is the lack of connection that many students feel after more than a year of virtual learning. Finally, because so many students were now so far behind, they might simply have been too discouraged to stay in class.

When that many students miss class, every student pays a price. According to the nonprofit organization Attendance Works, which helps schools address chronic absenteeism, "While chronic absence presents academic challenges for students not in class, when it reaches high levels in a classroom or school, all students may suffer because the resulting classroom churn hampers teachers' ability to engage all students and meet their learning needs."[42]

Some students will likely return. Parents who tried home schooling may want their children to be back in a classroom with other children. Children who simply disappeared because of technology problems or other family issues will also likely find their way back into a school building.

But many of these changes are likely to be permanent. Parents who have found a school that fits their child's learning needs, particularly if the public school they originally attended did not, are unlikely to return to the public schools. Since state funding formulas for public schools are heavily driven by average daily membership, that could result in a significant loss of funding.

For most school districts, state revenues make up the largest share of the budget. In most states, that revenue is heavily driven by student enrollment. When fewer students show up, fewer state dollars are allocated.

Some school districts will be better able to weather the enrollment losses than others. Some states will help cushion that decline by adopting a "hold harmless" provision, essentially holding state funding level for a year or two. Still, unless attendance rebounds, schools are likely to face significant budget challenges in the future.

CHAPTER 5

WAS IT ALWAYS THIS CONTENTIOUS?

> Human beings, who are almost unique in having the ability to learn from others, are also remarkable for their apparent disinclination to do so.
>
> —Douglas Adams

I was once lobbied while I was standing in the communion line. It was one of those awful years for the school budget. (Why are there so many more bad budget years than good ones?) One of the cuts proposed in the superintendent's budget was to shift the swim and dive program from a varsity sport to a club sport.

From an athletic point of view, the change would have made little difference. Kids could still swim competitively. They could still earn high school letters and be considered for college scholarships. Similarly, from a budget standpoint, the cuts were negligible. They were included, in all likelihood, as a symbol of the broader belt-tightening that was going on everywhere.

But the cost of renting the pool and paying the coaches would shift from the schools to the parents. Unsurprisingly, parents of kids in swim and dive hated the idea. They showed up everywhere—at budget hearings, at regular school board meetings, at high school swim meets. And, as it turned out, at my church.

So there I was, quietly waiting my turn, when a hand tugged at my sleeve. "I was wondering," the mom said, "if we could talk about swim and dive."

That story is helpful in understanding the reality of life for a local elected official. There's no buffer between you and your constituents. They see you *everywhere* and if you're any good at your job, they feel like they know you. They do not hesitate to bring up what's on their mind, whether you're standing in the produce section at the supermarket or, well, trying to approach the Throne of Grace.

These swim and dive parents were persistent, but they weren't threatening or mean. I gave the mom a look of disappointment. She understood that she might possibly have crossed some boundaries and turned her attention back to the Prayer Book.

Of course, polite behavior was not always the case, even thirty years ago. A former chair of the Fairfax County School Board needed police protection after receiving death threats when the county instituted Family Life Education. I once came close to filing a restraining order for a persistent parent who kept showing up at my house.

There was something about the chance encounters that may have helped lower the temperature for parent-school interactions. (Maybe they just meant I had to spend more time in the grocery store, talking math textbooks in the produce aisle.) But it was clear after parents had been inside for more than a year, the mood had changed.

One of the themes of this book is the increase in parent activism and anger during and after the pandemic. It provides much of the focus for chapter 6, where I note that in the Virginia election of 2021, parents came to be something of the It Girl of American politics.

When parents started showing up angry at school board meetings during 2021, some news stories covered the conflict as though there had never before been any school board protests anywhere, ever. In the wonderful words of Alexander Russo, who covers education reporting in the *Phi Delta Kappan*, too many news stories wrote about board protests as though they were writing about the television show *Squid Game*.

Yet pitched battles between parents and schools did not begin in Loudoun County, Virginia, in the summer of 2021. Instead, they have been a part of education history nearly from the beginning. On issues from sex education to evolution, from prayer in schools to the Pledge of Allegiance, America's public schools have often served as the turf on which larger social issues were fought.

"While the current slew of conflicts is notable, they're not really unusual or unique," Russo wrote. "There's a long history of school board controversies going back decades. Think sex ed, evolution, racial integration, or Ebonics. More recently, there have been school board protests over school closures, charter schools, Common Core, and teacher pay."[1]

It's worth taking a look at a few of those early conflicts, if only to put into some context the parental reaction to COVID school closures.

CINCINNATI'S BIBLE WARS

One of the earliest conflicts played out in Cincinnati, Ohio, in the mid-nineteenth century.[2] There, the city's public schools, like most public schools everywhere, began the school day with a reading of ten verses from the Bible.[3]

The practice likely began in Massachusetts, where schools had, after all, been established by the Puritans as a way to combat the "old deluder Satan." By the time Horace Mann, secretary of the Massachusetts board of education, began advocating for Bible reading, he had somehow made the argument that the practice was no longer a religious activity. Reading the Bible, as long as it was done "without comment," was presented nationwide as a nonsectarian practice.

By the mid-nineteenth century, public school students across the country all opened their day in much the same way. During the time when the nation was mostly a Protestant country, there was little objection to starting the day with a few Bible verses. But as the nation became more diverse, parents questioned whether this religious practice should be allowed in public schools. That led to a conflict that in Cincinnati came to be known as the Bible War of 1869.[4]

As early as the mid-1840s, non-Protestant Cincinnati parents came to the Protestant-dominated school board to voice their objections to Bible reading. To be clear, they were not opposed to starting the day with some religious reading. Rather, they were angry because, as Roman Catholics and Jews, they objected to reading the *King James* version of the Bible.

The city continued to attract immigrants, many Irish and German. Parental objections to the Bible reading increased. Bishop John Purcell began calling the city's public schools "Presbyterian schools," and worried aloud about the danger of public schools "in which the students are read to by the teacher from the heretical Bible and in which forbidden books are used which calumniate the Catholic religion."[5]

Under Purcell's leadership, the Catholic Church expanded the number of parochial schools in the city to ensure that Catholic children would receive appropriate religious training. Even so, many Catholic parents continued to exert pressure on the schools to change.

The school board's first response was to tell parents their concerns were unfounded. The 1840 *Report of the Board of Trustees and Visitors of the Common Schools* included this commentary: "The Bible or Testament, without notes or comments, are all read in the schools, and their moral precepts inculcated as principles of conduct and duty. No sectarian teachings are permitted and no requisitions are made of the pupils that come in conflict with the religious tenets of their parents, or of any religious sect or denomination."

Parents weren't reassured. Tempers continued to flare. Articles in the *Ohio Educational Monthly* extolled the importance of including the Bible in the curriculum. One author wrote, "education must have a sure foundation, and the teaching of the Bible is the only sure one; its morality is the true morality." Another stated that "the Bible's simplicity, beauty of style, moral code and promise of salvation make it ideal as a text book." On this basis, the writer concluded, the "Bible is not a sectarian book."

And if there was any question about which version of the Bible would be included, a report issued by the Western Literary Institute and College of Professional Teachers removed it. "We understand, then, by the word Bible, as used in the theme on which your committee are required to report, the common English version, or that effected by the public authority in the reign of James the First." The report was often cited by the pro-Bible members on the Cincinnati school board.

By the 1860s, the topic dominated news in the city. Newspapers carried editorials and cartoons. (And anyone who is concerned about Fake News today should read some of the polemics that were published on this issue.) Newspapers carried editorials and editorial cartoons.

Mass meetings were held. On September 28, the Friends of the Bible met in spacious Pike's Hall, also home to the Cincinnati Symphony Orchestra. As the *Cincinnati Enquirer* reported the next day, a parade of dignitaries sounded the same theme: without the Bible in schools, children would be Godless and immoral.[6]

On November 1, the school board voted 22 to 15 to exclude Bible readings from school opening practices. The next day, a group in opposition to the decision filed suit to prevent the board from implementing the decision. In their motion, the group charged that the action was against the law, an abuse of their authority, and would lead to the schools becoming a repository for Godlessness.

The plaintiffs won. In a 2–1 decision, the judges held that the Bible embodied the most profound system of human philosophy and that to deprive the schools of the Bible would leave them without God.

It's worth noting that this conflict not only divided Protestants from Roman Catholics. It also split more liberal Protestants from more conservative Protestants. That, of course, was a split that would occur again and again in fights over social issues.

Three years later, however, the decision was overturned by the Ohio Supreme Court.[7] The justices unanimously ruled that the Ohio Constitution took no position either in support of or in opposition to religion in the public schools. Therefore, the school board was within its authority to make decisions about the content of any morning exercises in schools. The decision noted that any power to authorize laws or policies over the subject rested with the legislature and that until laws mandating religious instruction were passed, the courts had no authority to interfere.

In that decision, Justice John Welch wrote, "The majority can protect itself. Constitutions are enacted for the very purpose of protecting the weak against the strong; the few against the many." It was not until 1963 that the US Supreme Court declared the practice unconstitutional.

THE SCOPES TRIAL

The issue of whose beliefs should be favored in the public schools continued to rile local communities. In the 1920s, the battle was over what would be taught in biology classes.

In 1922, House Bill 191 was introduced in the Kentucky General Assembly. As drafted, it would prohibit "the teaching in public schools and other public institutions of learning, Darwinism, atheism, agnosticism or evolution as it pertains to the origin of man."[8]

Teachers found guilty of violating the law could be fined between $50 and $5,000—between $825 and $82,500 today. They might also face jail time in the county jail for between ten days and a year. Institutions that allowed teachers to teach these offending "isms" could lose their charter and be fined up to $5,000. The bill was narrowly defeated, 42 to 41.[9] That pattern of blanket prohibitions coupled with fines and other penalties for teachers is one that has continued in many of the efforts to ban other controversial subjects.

Although the 1922 Kentucky effort did not pass, state legislators kept introducing legislation to ban the teaching of evolution. In 1925, the Tennessee State Legislature adopted a bill first proposed by Rep. John W. Butler to ban the teaching of evolution. It banned teaching "any theory that denies the story of the Divine Creation of man as taught in the Bible, and to teach instead that man has descended from a lower order of animals."[10]

The Butler Act further held that "any teacher found guilty of the violation of this Act, Shall be guilty of a misdemeanor and upon conviction, shall be fined not less than One Hundred ($100.00) Dollars nor more than Five Hundred ($500.00) Dollars for each offense." The legislation passed on March 13, 1925.

Like those who would later protest the teaching of Critical Race Theory without actually settling on a clear definition, the anti-evolutionists, wrote Jill

*Archbishop Purcell wrote a pastoral letter which the
Catholic Telegraph published on March 26, 1853,
in which he said if Catholics demanded their share
of the school funds, they would only be exercising
the right of every freeman. His letter invoked a
storm of protest from non-Catholics who called it
a plot to destroy the public schools.*

Figure 5.3. Increasing diversity in US suburbs

Lepore in an article in the *New Yorker*, were objecting to much more than a
biology textbook:

> When anti-evolutionists condemned "evolution," they meant something as
> vague and confused . . . Anti-evolutionists weren't simply objecting to Darwin,
> whose theory of evolution had been taught for more than half a century. They

were objecting to the whole Progressive package, including its philosophy of human betterment, its model of democratic citizenship, and its insistence on the interest of the state in free and equal public education as a public good that prevails over the private interests of parents.[11]

In Dayton, Tennessee, the biology textbook was George William Hunter's *A Civic Biology*. It described evolution as "the belief that simple forms of life on the earth slowly and gradually gave rise to those more complex and that thus ultimately the most complex forms came into existence."[12]

When the American Civil Liberties Union announced that it was looking for a way to challenge the law in court, a twenty-four-year-old teacher named John Scopes volunteered. His trial, featuring William Jennings Bryan defending the law and Clarence Darrow representing Scopes, became a national sensation.

That was entirely by design, according to a research project conducted by the Tennessee State Library and reported in an article in *Vox*. The town of Dayton was seeking publicity. The community leaders, including the superintendent of schools, recruited John Scopes to be the defendant.

The goal was to bring more people to town, and it was successful. "The Scopes trial," wrote Phil Edwards, "made the O. J. Simpson trial look downright low-profile."[13] Thousands of onlookers tried to jam their way into the courthouse. Famous visitors came to town. A July 5, 1925, front-page article in the *New York Times* called the city "Evolution Arena" and noted that a "circus atmosphere" pervaded the small town.[14]

Scopes was found guilty and fined, although the fine was later overturned on a technicality. The Butler law, however, was upheld by the Tennessee Supreme Court, and the law's supporters continued to press for adoption of textbooks that presented accurate science and allowed for academic freedom.

It was not until 1967 that Tennessee overturned the Butler law banning the teaching of evolution. The issue did not die, however. In 1981, the Arkansas legislature passed a law requiring public schools to give "balanced treatment" of creationism and evolution.

These two early examples of protests about what schools should teach include some hints of how the battles would come to be fought. First, policies would be proposed to ban some controversial topic. Punishments, particularly for teachers, would be outlined.

Rather than a battle of ideas, these fights usually included efforts to enlist the public at large in the controversy. Newspaper articles and cartoons, public meetings, and speeches were the early precursors to Facebook and Fox News.

Initially, policy makers would often try to tell parents that their concerns were groundless. That never seemed to work in the nineteenth century. Nor has it worked today.

CREATIONISM ON THE SCHOOL BOARD BALLOT

In 1995, when school board elections were first being held in Virginia, the creationism issue surfaced again. But this time, the proponents of teaching this religiously based doctrine in the public schools apparently wanted to keep their intentions under the radar.

I was a candidate in that race, which marked the first time since Massive Resistance that voters in Virginia could elect their school board members. Partly because it was the first time board members had been elected rather than appointed, and partly because it was Fairfax County, the school board race drew national attention. Candidates received questionnaires not only from the groups who had a direct interest in the outcome of the election, including the National Education Association and the American Federation of Teachers, but also from interest groups, including the National Rifle Association.

Four self-identified Christian conservative organizations, including the American Family Association, the Christian Coalition, Eagle Forum, and a group called HOPE (Help Our Parents Educate) distributed questionnaires asking candidates their views on a wide range of topics. Many touched on the hot-button issues of the day, including Goals 2000, homosexuality, and outcomes-based education. One of the questions on the survey asked if candidates would support the teaching of creationism. Twelve candidates expressed support for the idea.

Together, the four groups did not represent a large segment of the Fairfax County population. Their impact could potentially come in two ways. First, they could provide campaign workers, including those who would hand out sample ballots at the polls. Second, they would develop voter guides that would be handed out at conservative churches on the Sunday before the election.

On October 21, *Washington Post* reporter Robert O'Harrow published a story that shared the results of the questionnaire.[15] Creationism quickly came to dominate candidates' debates, news stories, and parent-to-parent discussions on the sidelines of soccer games. A CNN News story on the race said, "In a suburb of the nation's capital, an election for school board seats has turned into a contest over religion."[16]

I remember standing at the polls on Election Day. Voters I had never met would come up and ask, "Are you for or against creationism?" When I said I was opposed, they'd take my literature as they went into the polling place. In all, only two of the candidates who had supported creationism were elected.

It's likely the proponents of creationism anticipated this kind of defeat in highly educated suburban Fairfax County. Their goal was to encourage candidates instead to talk about teaching phonics or balancing the budget or anything except teaching creationism in high school science classes.

When the *Post* ran the story, the American Family Association tried to portray their interest as preventing censorship of curriculum, noting in a press release close to election day, "This question was asked as an indicator, to separate those who would censor the curriculum by excluding creation, from those who would be more broad-minded in this area."[17] Clearly, they had wanted the creationism issue, which proved to be very unpalatable to the education-minded parents in Fairfax County, under wraps.

In this first election, the candidates endorsed by the Democratic Party, all of whom opposed creationism, came out of the election with an 8–4 majority (two of the elected Republicans had also refused to endorse creationism).

But why, people asked me later, did candidates run for election with a party endorsement? The races were officially nonpartisan, and no party designation was listed on the ballot.

We knew from the beginning that one of the goals of some of the Christian conservatives in this election was to make the Fairfax County School Board a trophy and a representation of the kind of political power they could wield. We knew their candidates would have help in campaigning and, more importantly, would have a presence at every polling place all day on Election Day. Since the school board is typically a low-information race, simply having literature available to voters who have not made up their minds can generate a lot of votes.

We knew that it would be important to match that volunteer presence at the polls. Getting on the party's sample ballot was the most effective way to guarantee that presence. Our poll workers had sample ballots and copies of the *Washington Post* article available for anyone who wanted to read it. From the time the editorial was published, the outcome of the election was really never in doubt.

That is often the case with fights over curriculum. Parents are generally quite practical consumers of news. That was true in 1995 and it is still true today.[18] Once parents learned that some candidates might want to move toward a religious-based interpretation of science, they were clear about how they'd vote. But when parents don't have access to local news, the results can be quite different, as a 2021 controversy revealed.

THE PARENT BATTLES IN LOUDOUN COUNTY

Parents are not always the only ones who get exercised about what is being taught in the schools. In the leadup to the 2021 election for governor, Loudoun County, Virginia, became Ground Zero for a contentious round of protests that involved both parents and nonparents, and included people who lived in Loudoun County and those who did not. There was a time when anyone who watched cable news was aware of the latest salvo in an ongoing culture war.

In many ways, Loudoun, which was listed as the wealthiest county in the United States in 2021, represented the changes that had transformed America's suburbs from all-white enclaves to multicultural and diverse communities. Starting in 1965, when immigration quotas were relaxed, the United States had seen an influx of new Americans from Asia and Latin America. Most of them settled in the suburbs. At the same time, the percentage of African Americans living in the suburbs nearly doubled.[19] Figure 5.1 shows the increasing diversity of US suburbs in the last half century.[20]

Loudoun's growth was both tied to and reflective of these new patterns. The county's population quadrupled in thirty years. By 2021, roughly 25 percent of residents were immigrants, many of them from India and El Salvador. Although Loudoun was about 85 percent White in 2000, it was barely 60 percent White in 2020.

Between 1995 and 2020, the student population in Loudoun County Public Schools quadrupled, and a growing number of the new students reflected the changing makeup of the county's population. Instead of a majority of White students, the district's demographic profile was, by 2021, 43 percent White, 7 percent Black, 18 percent Hispanic, and 23 percent Asian and Pacific Islander.[21] Figure 5.2 shows the changes in the school's demographics between 2010 and 2021.

The new county residents were highly educated, with many working in the tech industry.

Reflecting national trends, voters with more education began shifting to the Democratic party. Loudoun was no longer a reliably Republican stronghold. In 2016, Hillary Clinton defeated Donald Trump 55 percent to 38 percent. In 2020, the Democratic margin grew, with voters strongly preferring Biden to Trump (61 percent to 37 percent). In 2021, the county was a target of both political parties in the election for Virginia's next governor.

Like many other suburban areas, Loudoun voters were not particularly partisan. Democratic political analyst Doug Sosnik observes, "Suburban voters remain resolutely practical-minded. They are concerned with raising children who can succeed in an increasingly complex, unpredictable society. They are worried about maintaining an economic status that, for many of these voters, is both relatively recent and precarious. These concerns often transcend racial or ethnic identity. These suburban voters are not attracted to the political extremism of either political party."[22]

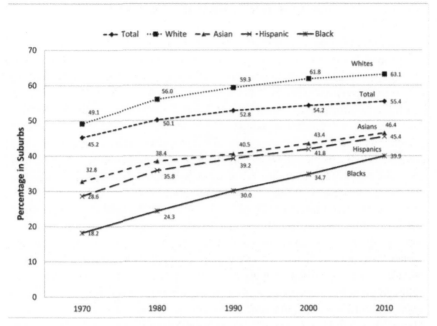

Figure 5.1. Increasing diversity in US suburbs

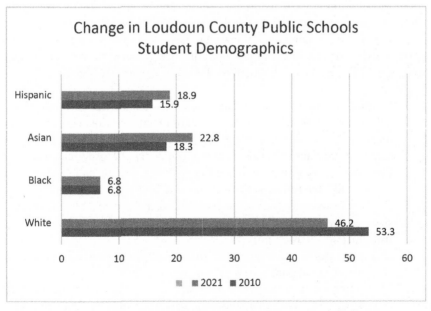

Figure 5.2. The changes in the school's demographics between 2010 and 2021

LOUDOUN'S HISTORY OF RACE

The county had a history of segregation that was not unlike many other parts of Virginia. It was one of the last school districts in the country to desegregate its schools.[23] Older Loudoun residents still remembered their own lived experience in segregated schools. That helped inform the conversation that began when the county branch of the NAACP filed a complaint with the Virginia Attorney General alleging a racially hostile environment in the school system.

Students of color said they had been subjected to racial slurs in class. Data showed that discipline referrals were disproportionately applied to students of color. Admission to the county's prestigious Academies of Loudoun program was not representative of the student population.

The report from the attorney general stated that the Office of Civil Rights (OCR) "found reason to believe that LCPS's policies and practices did, in fact, result in a disparate impact that harmed Black/African-American and Latinx/Hispanic students." In November 2020, the OCR sent a final determination to both parties. It included "reforms and commitments the Office believed must be undertaken in order to address the 'discriminatory disparate impact identified and help ensure equal opportunity for each student.'"[24] These included hiring consultants to monitor progress toward addressing the concerns.

To respond to the OCR letter, the county schools began conducting workshops for staff. The materials for the June 1, 2021, equity workshop were available online. Recommendations included results from a series of focus groups and interviews across the school division that had been conducted by consultants The Equity Collaborative. They highlighted five themes:[25]

1. Despite efforts from the division, school site staff, specifically principals and teachers, indicate a low level of racial consciousness and racial literacy. People are unclear and fearful on how to participate in conversations about race, let alone respond to racially charged incidents.
2. Educator focus groups indicated a desire to recruit and hire diverse school staff that reflect student racial and language backgrounds.
3. Economic diversity across the county/division complicates the discussions about race, leading many people to steer the conversation away from race to focus on poverty.
4. Discipline policies and practices disproportionately negatively impact students of color, particularly Black students.
5. Many English Learners, Black, Latinx, and Muslim students have experienced the sting of racial insults/slurs or racially motivated violent actions.

In all, these five findings were hardly controversial. School data backed up the fourth and fifth point, and research on student success has long confirmed the value of a diverse teaching staff.

But the discussion got swept into a larger, nationalized cultural battle. Parents who were already angry about the long-term school closures in Virginia saw the county's diversity training as an example of teaching Critical Race Theory. And that gave them something new to be mad about.

CRITICAL RACE THEORY

The battle about whether or not critical race theory (CRT) was being taught in classrooms took on a particular vitriol in Loudoun County. It was impossible to avoid discussion over whether the county's school children were being taught a racially divisive set of beliefs.

The issue quickly became a staple on Fox News, which ran seventy-eight segments on the topic between March and June, according to Media Matters, a generally progressive group that monitors media coverage. That accounted for more than four and a half hours of air time. The network's website linked to more than three hundred articles referencing Loudoun County and Critical Race Theory. (Cable news played an outsize role in this controversy.)

The language these news articles used was telling. Far too often, the words "suburban parents" were used as a shorthand way of saying "white parents." In Loudoun, where white students made up just 43 percent of the student population, suburban parents were more likely than not to be parents of color.

A *Washington Post* article quoted parent Rakelle Mullenix: "It seems as though Black and Brown voices were ignored, and the voices were centered on White parents and their concerns." She added, "I'm constantly hearing, 'Oh, no, suburban women, suburban moms and their vote.' And when I look around me and see these suburban moms and housewives, a lot of them look like me. But when I hear the conversations on the news, it doesn't sound like they're talking about me."[26]

That media coverage was amplified by a coordinated messaging program by think tanks like the Heritage Foundation and parent organizations largely funded and staffed by conservative activists. The Heritage Foundation released a toolkit it said would help parents use public information requests to determine whether CRT was being taught in their schools. "Our local schools are where the next generation of young minds are shaped, and citizens are molded. That's why it's so important to safeguard students from poisonous leftist teachings, including Critical Race Theory and transgender ideology," the tool kit began.[27]

Other national organizations also weighed in on the CRT controversy. They included:

- The Manhattan Institute, one of the most established conservative think tanks, published "Woke Schooling: A Toolkit for Concerned Parents" as part of a series on "woke" education that also included A Woke Education, and Woke Elementary, by anti-CRT leader Christopher Rufo.[28]
- Citizens Renewing America, founded by President Trump's former budget director Russell Vought, published a thirty-four-page guide for activists also in June, dedicated to "combating Critical Race Theory in your community."[29]
- Parents Defending Education was particularly active in Loudoun County. Their website included the two contracts that the LCPS signed with the Equity Collaborative. The website also included a download-able, fill-in-the-blanks resolution "prohibiting the teaching of Critical Race Theory."[30]
- Turning Point USA started School Board Watchlist, described as "America's only national grassroots initiative dedicated to protecting our children by exposing radical and false ideologies endorsed by school boards and pushed in the classroom. The website published the names and photographs of school board members around the country.[31]
- The 1776 Project, a political action committee, backed school board candidates nationwide who oppose antiracist curricula. The group raised over $420,000 and disbursed nearly $300,000 between January 1 and September 30, 2021, according to the Federal Elections Commission.[32]
- Moms for Liberty offered parents a step-by-step guide on how to sub-mit an open records request. The group also orchestrated campaigns to ban books, mostly by authors of color or LGBTQ authors, from school libraries.[33]

Despite the hue and cry, there was no real consensus about what CRT even was. In this book, here is the definition: CRT is primarily taught in graduate schools, starting in the 1970s. Generally it starts with a belief that laws and practices, and not just individual discrimination, are involved with racial disparities. When banks drew red lines around certain areas and refused to lend homeowners in those areas money to purchase housing, those decisions were allowed by the legal system of the time. It was not just a few bankers who were bad actors. Rather, it was the entire system that kept families who owned property in those areas from accumulating wealth.

In education, CRT generally involves looking at how policies and practices in K–12 schools contribute to racial inequalities in education. That might include a look at racially segregated schools or differences in how students of color and white students are disciplined. CRT might also involve an examination of admission to gifted programs or advanced classes.

But CRT opponents tended to use a much more expansive definition. Activist Christopher Rufo intentionally set out to blur the definition, hoping to turn it into a catch phrase meaning any teaching about race that made any white person feel uncomfortable. "Its connotations are all negative to most middle-class Americans, including racial minorities, who see the world as 'creative' rather than 'critical,' 'individual' rather than 'racial,' 'practical' rather than 'theoretical,'" he said to a reporter from the *New Yorker.* He wanted the phrase to seem "hostile, academic, divisive, race-obsessed, poisonous, elitist, anti-American."[34]

Tiffany Justice, a cofounder of Moms for Liberty and a former school board member in Florida, listed the programs her anti-CRT group was opposing: "I call it alphabet soup laced with snake oil. It's CRT, DEI, SEL, this word salad of acronyms that are being shoved into every crack and crevice of American education."[35]

So at various times, CRT was used to describe assigning a Toni Morrison novel to a high school English class. Some parents charged that a book about Ruby Bridges, the first Black child to integrate an all-white elementary school (the book didn't have enough "redemption") was CRT. Some parents complained about lessons on Martin Luther King.

On the night after the election, Fox News host Tucker Carlson said, "I've never figured out what 'Critical Race Theory' is, to be totally honest, after a year of talking about it."[36]

A *Washington Post* story on the protests against CRT at the Loudoun County School Board included a photograph of a woman holding a sign that read:

PROTECT CHILDREN
NO UNISEX BATHROOMS
NO SEXUAL LESSONS
NO INDOCTRINATION
NO CHEMICAL BLOCKERS
NO MANDATED VAX
NO CRT.[37]

Frankly, from a strictly political perspective, the blurry definition worked well for the anti-CRT crowd. The Virginians who still talked about the "War of Northern Aggression" and plastered the Stars and Bars on their vehicles could see a move against CRT as reasserting white supremacy. But centrists could also see it as simply a way to dial back on some of the most divisive training conducted with the goal of promoting diversity, equity, and inclusion (DEI).

Which some of these parents knew firsthand. Following the national conversation about race that arose following George Floyd's murder in Minneapolis, many companies and organizations sought to provide DEI training to their employees. In fact, Christopher Rufo, the political activist who elevated CRT into a national issue, first learned about the issue when a Seattle city employee leaked him documents taken from a city-sponsored (and mandatory) equity training program.[38]

Certainly the desire to provide an opportunity to examine beliefs and practices, particularly in the period of racial reckoning that followed the George Floyd murder in Minneapolis, was important. But an honest appraisal would conclude that some of the training provided was, well, uneven.

There were few rigorous evaluations of the organizations conducting the training sessions, or of the materials they were using as part of the training. Some of those early programs seem in retrospect to have been designed to create controversy. One popular handout was a Bridging Cultures Framework. It emphasized that white culture promoted individualism, but that "color group" culture was collective.

Among the characteristics of white supremacy culture were "perfectionism, a sense of urgency, defensiveness, valuing quantity over quality, worship of the written word, belief in only one right way, paternalism, either/or thinking, power hoarding, fear of open conflict, individualism, belief that I'm the only one (who can do this 'right'), the belief that progress is bigger and more, a belief in objectivity, and claiming a right to comfort."[39]

A *Scientific American* evaluation of training programs found "consistent evidence that bias training done the 'wrong way' (think lukewarm diversity training) can actually have the opposite impact, inducing anger and frustration among white employees. What this all means is that, despite the widespread calls for implicit bias training, it will likely be ineffective at best; at worst, it's a poor use of limited resources that could cause more damage and exacerbate the very issues it is trying to solve."[40] That appears to be what happened in Loudoun.

Parents Defending Education obtained one of the invoices submitted by The Equity Collaborative to LCPS. It asked for reimbursement for "Equity Leadership Coaching," and included the explanation "Coaching support for LCPS leaders—follow up meetings focused on Critical Race Theory Development May 2020.[41]

Parents started showing up at school board meetings to rail about how children were being indoctrinated and made to feel ashamed of being white. Two groups, the Virginia Project and Parents Against Critical Theory, held a webinar called "What Is CRT and Its Impact on Loudoun County Schools?"[42] The Equity Collaborative website was featured in that workshop.

The organization Fight for Schools, led by a Loudoun father who was also a former official in the Trump administration, filed recall petitions against six LCPS school board members. One, Leesburg representative Beth Barts, ultimately resigned. The others awaited a trial (in Virginia, recalls are handled through the courts rather than through the electoral process). A similar effort to recall school board members in neighboring Fairfax County failed.

In fact, most public school parents want their children to learn accurate information about race in school. A *USA Today*/Ipsos poll found that more than 60 percent of American parents want their kids to learn about the ongoing effects of slavery and racism as part of their education.[43] Yet in the same poll, fewer than four in ten wanted their children to learn about Critical Race Theory.

Another poll found that when the term "Critical Race Theory" is removed from the question, most Americans actually believe in its central tenet. When asked "How big a problem is racism in our society today?" an overwhelming majority (70 percent) agreed, with 43 percent saying it is a "big problem."

Respondents were also asked whether they believed that "racism is only a problem with individuals who are racist, or is it a problem that exists within the country's organizational, societal, and legal structure?" (This, of course, is close to a definition of Critical Race Theory.) Just 29 percent said it was an individual problem, while 59 percent said it was a sign of a "broader, structural problem." See figure 5.3.

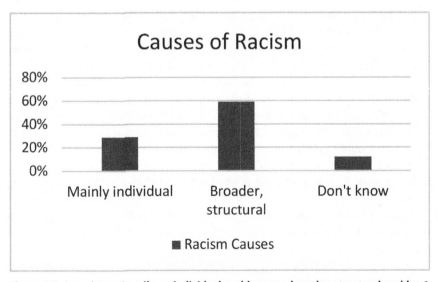

Figure 5.3. Is racism primarily an individual problem or a broader, structural problem?
Source: YouGov poll

Clearly, what something is *called* helps determine how people feel about it. Remember the big disparity between those who supported "Obamacare" and those who were in favor of the "Affordable Care Act."

Were the Loudoun County Public Schools teaching "Critical Race Theory" to students? An examination of the district's curriculum standards, as well as its social studies scope and sequence documents, indicates they clearly were not. But when the term had become so blurry as to be almost meaningless, it was hard to sort out what parents might be objecting to. And it was hard for the school system to say that they were not teaching CRT when their own invoice acknowledged that administrators were receiving CRT coaching support.

The *Washington Post* summarized board chair Linda Orr's comments. The pandemic, she said, had forced parents inside and online, where they stewed in fear and frustration, then united in thousands-strong Facebook groups dedicated to advocacy regarding mask mandates and school reopenings. And when the CRT debate arose, all that "functioned like a lit match thrown on a rag soaked in gasoline."[44]

BOARD FACES A SECOND CONTROVERSIAL ISSUE

A note here before starting this section. It is long and filled with quotes from both state law and school board policy. If it were on the internet, many people would simply describe it as TL/DR (too long; didn't read). But having the exact language in policy is important when this topic, sexual assault of a student, is under discussion. Clearly, such a sensitive issue is going to evoke strong feelings. In Loudoun, this incident eventually generated an attorney general's investigation into how the county had handled the assault.

But even people who think the school system did a poor job of handling both the law enforcement part of the assault and the communications part of the assault, and I am one of them, should understand that it was a complicated and difficult situation under ideal circumstances. And the circumstances in Loudoun County in 2021 were anything but ideal.

As the school board was addressing concerns about school closures and CRT, it was also dealing with a new state law that added a new section, *§ 22.1–23.3. Treatment of transgender students; policies* to the Code of Virginia. The law required school boards to adopt policies to address issues relating to the "treatment of transgender students in public elementary and secondary schools."[45]

In complying with the law, the school board proposed a new policy that included these two sections.

A. Student Identification—Names and Pronouns.

LCPS staff shall allow gender-expansive or transgender students to use their chosen name and gender pronouns that reflect their gender identity without any substantiating evidence, regardless of the name and gender recorded in the student's permanent educational record. School staff shall, at the request of a student or parent/legal guardian, when using a name or pronoun to address the student, use the name and pronoun that correspond to their gender identity.

B. Access to Facilities.

All students are entitled to have access to restrooms and locker rooms that are sanitary, safe, and adequate, so that they can comfortably and fully engage in their school programs and activities. Students should be allowed to use the facility that corresponds to their gender identity. While some transgender students will want that access, others may want alternatives that afford more privacy. Taking into account existing school facilities, administrators should take steps to designate gender-inclusive or single-user restrooms commensurate with the size of the school.[46]

The policy was a particular hot-button issue because of a recent sexual assault in the girls' bathroom of one of the county's high schools. The perpetrator had reportedly been wearing a skirt on the day of the assault. (Parents described the student as "gender fluid" and argued that they wore the skirt to gain access to the women's bathroom. They also argued that the new transgender policy made it easier for the perpetrator to carry out the attack.[47] In fact, the policy had not yet taken effect.

Further, the victim's father was furious with school officials because he believed that nothing was being done to prosecute the attacker. A local journalist obtained police dispatch records that strongly disputed that.[48]

Sexual assaults are among the most difficult issues for schools to address in public. The normal goal of protecting an individual student's privacy is even more important when a student is also a sexual assault victim and when both parties involved are underage.

The assailant had committed a previous assault and had been allowed to continue attending school, although he had been transferred to a different high school. That was due at least in part to new Title IX regulations prohibiting the county from disciplining a student without following the law's grievance process. That required a full, and time-consuming, investigation.

When the regulations were released, Education Secretary Betsy DeVos had supported them, saying, "Too many students have lost access to their education because their school inadequately responded when a student filed a complaint of sexual harassment or sexual assault."[49] With apparently no irony intended, the Department rolled out a set of regulations making it harder to discipline students for sexual assault as "historic action to strengthen Title IX protection for all students."

Washington Senator Patty Murray, vice chair of the Senate Health, Education, Labor, and Pensions Committee sounded a cautionary note. "This rule will make it that much harder for a student to report an incident of sexual assault or harassment—and that much easier for a school to sweep it under the rug."[50]

In a community already divided by the issue of CRT, news of an unreported sexual assault led to a social media firestorm and clearly pointed to a toxic and very public blowup.

The issue boiled over at a board meeting in June, when the school board was debating the proposed regulation on transgender students. As was their usual practice, the board allowed citizens to sign up to address the board. Well over 250 parents signed up. But many more showed up at the meeting. They shouted and chanted "Shame on You." When the chair called for order, they continued to chant and wave signs.

The audience members grew louder. Repeated requests by the chair failed to quiet the crowd. In the end, two members of the audience were arrested, including a man named Scott Smith. A photograph of Mr. Smith, lip bleeding and hands cuffed behind his back, being pulled out of the meeting went viral as a sign of the kind of anger being unleashed at school board meetings. Unreported at the time was the fact that Mr. Smith was the father of the victim of the sexual assault, and that he blamed the policy for the assault.

The issue exploded on social media and even in Congress. Senator Tom Cotton, in a Judiciary Committee hearing with Attorney General Merrick Garland, charged that the victim "was raped in a bathroom by a boy wearing girls' clothes and the Loudoun County School Board covered it up because it would interfere with their transgender policy during pride month."[51] Only the first half of that sentence was true. There was a sexual assault. It was in a bathroom. And the assailant was wearing girls' clothes.

It was not until a court hearing in October that the public learned that the two students had previous a relationship and that they had previously engaged in consensual sexual encounters. The young woman was the victim of an assault, but it was not a random assault. Rather, hers was a case of relationship violence, which is sadly not uncommon. A judge did find "sufficient evidence to sustain the charges," the equivalent of a guilty finding.

The superintendent announced many changes to the district's discipline policies and relationship with the County Sheriff. He also noted that the system would advocate for changes to the Title IX regulations. Finally, he agreed that the school system would release as much information as it could in real time.

The board agreed to vote on the policy at its regular August 10 meeting. At that meeting, the policy was approved by a vote of 7–2.

STATE LEGISLATURES GET INVOLVED

A century after the Scopes trial, the country was again living through a wave of fights about what school children should and should not learn. Across the country, state legislators weighed in on how teachers should help students learn about race in American history.

Let me just say from the outset, as someone who spent an entire decade in a state legislature, that it is a very bad idea for legislators to write curriculum. The efforts usually are knee-jerk reactions to some issue that has roiled up a group of voters. And the proposed legislative solutions, instead of helping, often end up making it harder for schools, for parents, and for students to deal with the issue.

One of the best examples came in Virginia after a freshman Delegate, Wren Williams, decided that he needed to introduce a bill to combat the dangers of Critical Race Theory in Virginia. House Bill 781[52] would have amended the Code of Virginia by adding a new § 22.1-208.03, which was designed, as the first line of the bill said, to prohibit "certain instructional practices." And while Critical Race Theory was not specifically called out in the legislation, there could be little doubt that was what was targeted.

Under § A (ii) of the legislation, teachers could not discuss issues related to race, religion, ethnicity, or sex if the discussion suggested that any individual was *"inherently racist, sexist, or oppressive, whether consciously or unconsciously."*

The bill also specified in § A (viii) that no school training programs could teach that *meritocracy, punctuality, proper language usage, free markets, and traits such as strong work ethic are racist or sexist or were created by members of a particular race to oppress members of another race.*

It might have passed but for what was probably intended to be the most innocuous part of the legislation, § B (3), enumerated all the content that *could* be taught in Virginia schools. Referred to as "founding documents," the list included "the Declaration of Independence, the Constitution, excerpts from the Federalist Papers, the writings of the Founding Fathers and Alexis de Tocqueville's classic Democracy in America." And, perhaps in an effort to ensure that the list would include at least one document authored by a person of color, the list also included "the first debate between Abraham Lincoln and Frederick Douglass."

There was, of course, no such debate. In the Senate election of 1858, Abraham Lincoln challenged sitting senator Stephen Douglas to a series of debates across the state of Illinois. Because a major focus of the debates was on the issue of slavery, they are critical to understanding how the nation's policy on this issue evolved. Although Lincoln lost the Senate election, he did win the presidency two years later.

And while in the White House, he did meet with noted abolitionist and former enslaved person Frederick Douglass. But it would be a real stretch to call that meeting a debate.

Reaction to the introduction of the bill was swift and, well, not kind. University of Virginia professor Larry Sabato and Norman Ornstein of the American Enterprise Institute, had this Twitter exchange:

Larry Sabato ✔ @LarrySabato · 14h
I hope we can also include a discussion of the memorable Jimmy Carter-Henry Ford debates. And certainly, add the George W. Bush-Lesley Gore face-offs. Gore was so gracious when she conceded. I still remember her first line: "It's my party and I'll cry if I want to."
twitter.com/LarrySabato/st...

Norman Ornstein ✔ @NormOrnstein · 13h   ...
Replying to @LarrySabato and @EricKleefeld
I can't believe you made that mistake. It was Jimmy Carter vs Tennessee Ernie Ford!

🗨 4   ⟲ 5   ♡ 65   ⬆

Twitter Exchange

Although the Division of Legislative Services took responsibility for the error, it was withdrawn.

BOOK BANS

The anger in Loudoun County was a harbinger of other angry outbursts nationwide. Politicians have known for years that angry voters are loyal voters. A study of voters in Colorado found that anger is now actually most effective on more moderate voters. "The really far left and right are already so amped up," said Carey Stapleton, a researcher at the University of Colorado.

"But these weakly-aligned partisans who are notoriously less likely to participate in elections were more susceptible to changing their emotions."[53]

Certainly anger over Donald Trump's election spurred an increase in
Democratic turnout in 2017 and 2018. Today, angry Republican voters are
essential to the GOP electoral strategy. And if the party's electoral success depends on motivating angry voters, there will always need to be a
new outrage.

Once the CRT heat seemed to burn off, the new tactic was book bans.
A 2022 report by PEN America, an organization dedicated to literary and
free expression, found an enormous uptick in decisions to ban books in
school libraries and classrooms in the United States from July 1, 2021, to
March 31, 2022.

In many cases, these were cases of school administrators responding to
complaints from parents about specific books—often books by LGBTQ
authors or authors of color. But in other cases, state legislatures began trying
their hand, as in the Virginia case described above, at determining what can
be taught and read in schools.

The Supreme Court has ruled on book bans. In Board of Education, Island
Trees Union Free School District v. Pico, the Supreme Court stated: "Our
Constitution does not permit the official suppression of ideas." The ruling
affirmed the "special characteristics" of the school library, making it "especially appropriate for the recognition of the First Amendment rights of students," including the right to access information and ideas.

The central holding of *Pico*, on page 872 of the decision, was "[L]ocal
school boards may not remove books from school library shelves *simply
because they dislike the ideas contained in those books and seek by their
removal to prescribe what shall be orthodox in politics, nationalism, religion,
or other matters of opinion*"[54] (emphasis added).

As uncomfortable as it is to live through a challenged book process, which
sometimes confronted the school board on which I served, it is possible.
Having solid policies on how to proceed when a book is challenged, *and then
following those policies*, is the key to reaching an appropriate outcome. PEN
America says that its review found that just 4 percent of the 1,586 individual
book bans have been the result of processes that began with the filing of formal challenges to library or classroom materials by community members.[55]

The National Coalition Against Censorship and the American Library
Association have developed clear guidelines on how to proceed.[56] The recommendations include requiring a written statement for formal reconsideration
of a book, creation of a committee that includes educators and community
members who are trained in issues including the First Amendment, and
a recommendation that books remain in circulation while the decision is
in process.

To these, I would add conditions developed by Fairfax County: that once a book has been through the process of reconsideration, it cannot be brought up again for a period of time, which in FCPS is three years; that only persons with standing (parents whose children are in the grades where the materials would be used or staff members who would teach those materials) can file complaints, and that complainants must have read the book they are challenging.[57]

When state legislatures began their efforts to ban "divisive content," many of the bills included language so vague that educators worried about their ability to discuss topics like slavery and segregation in their classrooms. In response, the College Board, who develop and certify Advanced Placement classes in high schools, made its position clear.

First, the College Board emphasized that AP classes are optional. "Parents and students freely choose to enroll in AP courses. Course descriptions are available online for parents and students to inform their choice. Parents do not define which college-level topics are suitable within AP courses; AP course and exam materials are crafted by committees of professors and other expert educators in each field."

Then the organization outlined that the materials in AP courses are thus not optional. For example, *The Bluest Eye* by Toni Morrison (a book that has frequently been pulled from schools) is sometimes one of the texts included in an AP literature class. If a teacher chose not to assign it, or if a school board or school administrator prohibited it, then the course would lose its AP license and the AP designation would be removed from the students' transcripts.

When the school board in Placentia-Yorba Linda School District, California, considered a ban on CRT in the schools, students and parents raised the College Board's statement. Students and parents expressed concerns that because AP classes are one way to raise their grade point average, any limit on the number of AP classes they would take might make them less competitive in California's highly competitive college application process. They were also worried that the ban would limit what they learned.

The district responded quickly. "The district has no intention to proceed with any action that would inhibit its ability to continue to offer AP courses and content," district spokeswoman Alyssa Griffiths said.[58] However, the resolution banning CRT passed by a vote of 3–2 at the April 5 school board meeting.[59]

Parents are already organizing to help schools keep books on shelves. The advocacy group Red Wine & Blue has organized a campaign called Book Ban Busters.[60] The group encourages suburban women to get involved locally, hosting read-ins, serving on review committees, and donating banned books.

In Round Rock, Texas, a group of Black moms has organized to make sure school libraries and reading lists include books that depict people of color and LGBTQ individuals. The group gathered thousands of signatures to keep the book *Stamped: Racism, Antiracism, and You* on a school-approved reading list.[61]

CONCLUSION

Even after children were back in schools, anger at the schools continued. Battles over whether children should wear masks reached such a fever pitch that in Page County, Virginia, one mother threatened to "bring every single gun loaded and ready" if masks continued to be required.[62]

Anger certainly was a motivation in two elections held shortly after in-person schooling was resumed. Increasingly, anger showed up as a motivating force in both elections. Those elections are discussed in chapter 6.

CHAPTER 6

PARENTS AS THE "IT GIRL" IN TWO EARLY ELECTIONS

I could be the It Girl, can't you see
I could be the face on a magazine

—From *It Girl* by Raye Zaragoza

School closures lasted longer in the United States than in most high-income countries, and much longer in blue jurisdictions than in red ones. Nearly a year after schools had first closed, roughly half of all school children in the United States were still only able to attend school virtually, according to the website Burbio (as shown in figure 3.1). In February 2021, the six states with the largest concentrations of school districts still operating entirely virtually, were California, Maryland, New Mexico, Oregon, Virginia, and Washington.

By January of 2021, there was a growing scientific consensus that most children could return to school. Many teachers were vaccinated, although precise numbers here, like so many other things in COVID, were hard to find. The most accurate data likely comes from the Centers for Disease Control, which reported in April that 80 percent of teachers, school staff, and childcare workers had received at least one shot.[1]

And yet schools did not reopen in many places. Why?

Politics, you will be shocked to learn, played a role. As with nearly every other aspect of how this country dealt with a global health crisis, the governmental response to COVID has never not been political.

In states that voted for Donald Trump, schools reopened much sooner in the 2020–2021 school year than states that voted for Biden. Chad Aldeman, an education researcher and a public school parent, calculated that his first-grade son, a student in Fairfax, Virginia, was scheduled to receive less than half a typical school year's worth of in-person time with educators in 2020–2021.[2] Using data from Burbio, *The 74* calculated that students in states that voted for Donald Trump received 134 days of in-person instruction during the 2020–2021 school year, compared with 67.7 days in states that voted for Joe Biden.[3]

Collective bargaining was also an issue. In San Francisco, contract negotiations over whether and when to return to school effectively kept the schools closed for the entire school year. In Seattle, talks with the teacher's union also stalemated over when students could return to their classroom.

In mid-February of 2021, the King County (Seattle) schools announced they would bring back no students older than second grade to in-person learning for the remainder of the school year. In making the announcement, a school spokesperson reported that negotiations between the district and the union were unlikely to reach an agreement on expanding in-person learning during the current school year beyond the early grades.[4]

That may have been the tipping point for Governor Jay Inslee. On March 12, exactly one year after schools in the state had closed, he issued an executive order *requiring* schools to open to elementary students by April 5 and to secondary students by April 19.[5] At the time he issued the proclamation, the Seattle schools were providing in-person instruction to 150 students.[6]

Those extended closures meant that families in some late-opening states and districts spent more than a year online. For many professionals, work went online. School was online. Staying connected with friends and family also often became a virtual endeavor, with family Zoom chats and virtual book groups taking the place of in-person gatherings. And of course social media became a place to share frustrations, Netflix recommendations, and the home baker's latest efforts to produce a sourdough bread. Chapter 3 details how parents used Facebook to set up pandemic pods with nearby families.

It's not surprising, then, that parents also began seeking or creating online groups for support during virtual schooling. Unsurprisingly, researchers found that parents were more likely to use social media to help them relieve their anxiety.[7] In the days before a vaccine, parents often shared information on alternative health measures that might keep their kids safe. (Later, according to a study by George Washington University, these links to alternative health sites became primary channels for some parents to disseminate anti-vaccine and anti-mask information.)[8]

Parents also paid more attention to education news. The Hewlett Foundation surveyed parents in 2020 and 2021 to learn which topics they considered most important. Education topped the list, with interest in the subject growing between 2020 and 2021. Figure 6.1 shows the importance parents placed on this news coverage.

And honestly, a lot of parents just got mad. In an NPR Politics podcast, reporter Susan Davis said that in some ways, 2021 felt a lot like 2010 with the rise of the Tea Party. "I think there is very broad parental anger that children have not been treated well in the pandemic, that the effects of pandemic living

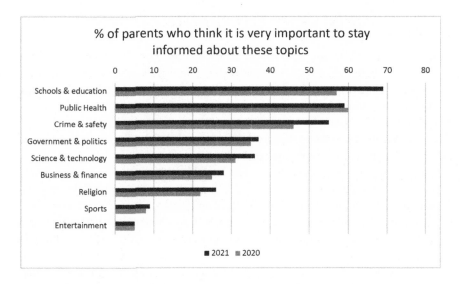

Figure 6.1. Parents' interest in various news topics

From J. Holcomb, T. Hartson, Y. Kim, et al., *Keeping Up with the Ed Beat: How News Habits, Racial Identity, and a Public Health Crisis Have Shaped Parents' Experience with Education News,* William & Flora Hewlett Foundation, February 2022, retrieved from https://calvin.edu/centers-institutes/center-for-social-research/ projects-services/education-news/files/Education%20News%20Survey%20Report%2020220216.pdf.

on children have been profound," she offered. "Anger is a huge motivator for voters."

As was the case during the Tea Party, in 2010, "You would talk to voters. And, like, they were just mad. The anger's so palpable. . . . When you talk to voters that are that mad, they're just going to vote. Like, anger is just such a motivating force, especially when you're talking about actual policies that you think have affected your children."[9]

Many parents channeled their anger into politics. Parents tuned in to the meetings of their local school boards to learn about plans for reopening schools. The angry confrontations described in chapter 5 in Loudoun County now happened everywhere. Then they turned to other parents to organize a response to what they were hearing.

That led to increased parent participation in elections. Two early elections, the Virginia governor's election in 2021 and a recall election for three San Francisco school board members, illustrate how parents played a role. Both elections revealed some important shifts in how parents would respond to school closures at the ballot box.

VIRGINIA'S 2021 ELECTION FOR GOVERNOR

Let's begin with a little election math. If you are a party that has been losing elections, there are only two ways to start winning. You can persuade some people who have voted for the other party to switch and vote for you. Or you can gin up enough excitement in your own partisans that all of them, every last one, will turn out to vote.

The Virginia election was seen as an example of the first strategy. In fact, it was the second strategy that worked.

(Cynics might point out that there is a third alternative. You can simply suppress the vote of your opponents or flood the campaign with disinformation. But this chapter focuses on the legal and appropriate ways to campaign.)

Because Virginia has off-year elections, it has become a state where both parties try out campaign messages and get-out-the-vote (GOTV) techniques in the year following a presidential election (with an eye to then taking those that work nationwide for the off-year Congressional elections). I sometimes describe Virginia in those increasingly nationalized elections as resembling Spain during the Spanish Civil War—the territory on which many outsiders were working out their plans for future battles.[10]

As early as 2001, Republicans field-tested a GOTV program developed by Karl Rove that came to be known as the 72-Hour Project. It was used in the 2002 and 2004 Congressional elections and was widely credited with giving the party a strategic and technological edge that helped hold the House and (with help from Sen. Jeffords) the Senate.

In 2009, the GOP capitalized on the unpopularity of the Affordable Care Act (ACA). Campaign messaging drove home the idea that the ACA would cost Virginians jobs. The Republican candidate for governor, Bob McDonnell, campaigned on the slogan "Bob's for Jobs" and won in a landslide. No one was surprised to see those same themes used nationally the next year as the GOP gained sixty-three seats in the House and six in the Senate.

In other words, it was pretty predictable that in 2021, Virginia would again be the site of a ground war on messaging. The election did not go according to the script, however. While the Republican candidate Glenn Youngkin telegraphed from a very early stage that he thought the election would be about Critical Race Theory, it actually had much more to do with school closures.

A brief digression here to explain why Virginia even *has* an election in the year following a presidential contest. These every-year elections are a remnant of the Jim Crow laws that were enacted by the Byrd Machine, which controlled Virginia politics from the 1890s into the 1960s. They were clearly intended to make sure the Right Sort of Person voted in the state elections, and they've been quite effective. Even-year elections tend to attract more

Virginia's Contrary History of Presidential/Gubernatorial Elections

Presidential Election Year	Winner and Party	Virginia Governor's Election Year	Winner and Party
1976	Jimmy Carter—D	1977	John Dalton—R
1980	Ronald Reagan—R	1981	Chuck Robb—D
1984	Ronald Reagan—R	1985	Gerald Baliles—D
1988	George H. W. Bush—R	1989	Douglas Wilder—D
1992	Bill Clinton—D	1993	George Allen—R
1996	Bill Clinton—D	1997	Jim Gilmore—R
2000	George W. Bush—R	2001	Mark Warner—D
2004	George W. Bush—R	2005	Tim Kaine—D
2008	Barack Obama—D	2009	Bob McDonnell—R
2012	Barack Obama—D	2013*	Terry McAuliffe—D
2016	Donald Trump—R	2017	Ralph Northam—D
2020	Joseph Biden—D	2021	Glenn Youngkin—R

voters of color and young voters, who tend to vote more Democratic. But in the odd-year elections, a smaller electorate tends to be older and whiter.

These off-year elections also allowed the conservative Virginia Democrats to avoid the taint of appearing on the ballot with more liberal national Democrats.

Those off-year campaigns also tended to excite the supporters of whichever candidate had just lost the presidential race. Following the election of George H. W. Bush in 2000 and 2004, Virginians elected Democratic governors Mark Warner and Tim Kaine. In 2009 following the election of Barack Obama as president, Virginia voters chose Republican Bob McDonnell as governor. The 2017 campaign for governor, which followed the Trump election, was a big win for Democrat Ralph Northam.

The sole exception to this trend in more than forty years? Terry McAuliffe, who won as a Democrat in 2013 following the reelection of Barack Obama in 2012. He was trying to repeat hstory in 2021. Figure 6.2 shows Virginia's contrary history of governor's elections.

The election of Donald Trump helped shift the partisan energy on the Democratic side into overdrive, electing Ralph Northam as governor by the largest victory margin in nearly forty years. In 2018, three new Democratic women were elected to Congress. In 2019, both houses of the General

Assembly flipped to Democratic control, the Virginia House of Delegates for the first time in a generation.

In the 2020 presidential election, Joe Biden defeated Donald Trump by more than ten points in Virginia. Some pundits—and, frankly, some Democrats—mentally moved Virginia into the "Safe D" column on their electoral score cards.

As a candidate for office and an elected official, I learned one lesson early: if you were a Democrat, you were going to win on the education issue about 99 percent of the time. There were plenty of other issues where Republicans had an advantage—cutting taxes, for example, or fighting crime. But when asked which party they trusted most on education, voters consistently named the Democrats.

In fact, the issue was such a given that many national polls had stopped even asking the question. The *Washington Post* noted that NBC News-Wall Street Journal polling had showed Democrats with an edge on the issue in every survey it had done since 1989. On only five occasions in the two dozen polls had the Democratic advantage been less than double digits, and it never dropped below a six-point lead.[11]

That changed in the Virginia 2021 election.

The leadup to the 2021 election for governor in Virginia featured newspaper headlines that highlighted education as a key issue in the race. "Education Clashes Shape Virginia Governor's Race," said the *Christian Science Monitor.* "Education Takes Center Stage in Va. Governor's Race," reported the *New York Post.* Even Utah's *Deseret News* highlighted the education fight going on in Virginia.

And this time, when voters said education was their top issue, they really seemed to mean it. In the past, candidates for state and local office noticed a disconnect between what voters often *said* about education (that it was a top concern, that it would drive their election decision) and what they ended up doing once they were in the voting booth (voting primarily on the basis of jobs or taxes or health care). Even at the local level, where most important decisions about schools are made, education was rarely the number one issue on voters' minds.

As noted in chapter 5, parents were credited with the Virginia wins. Critical Race Theory was seen as the ticket to encouraging suburban parents to switch their votes and support Republicans. The Cato Institute suggested "Parents Are the New Electoral Power Players." A *Wall Street Journal* editorial on the day after the election was headlined, "Youngkin Makes the GOP the Parents' Party." Fox News carried a story titled "Virginia Moms and Dads Say Youngkin Victory a Win for Parental Rights."

Suddenly, parents were the new "It Girls" of American politics. The *New York Times* story on ad spending in the race suggested, "Schools have quickly climbed to the forefront of national political scraps."[12]

Later, the McAuliffe campaign said it had known something was up from the start. "While the conventional wisdom is that Democrats should maintain an advantage on education, we actually found that Democrats largely were underwater on education at the start of the race. Given the fatigue many Virginians faced after school closures and COVID, McAuliffe started the race at a disadvantage on education," the campaign wrote in a post-election memo released on November 5. "Our polling back in July saw Youngkin with a one-point advantage over McAuliffe with education which held true throughout the rest of the campaign."[13]

Which makes the campaign's tepid response, even as polling was showing the issue helping motivate undecided voters, more puzzling. Between September and October, education rose by nine points to become the most important issue in the race.[14] That was particularly true for late deciders. A poll by Democrats for Education Reform (DFER) and Murmuration, a company that conducted national polling for the Biden-Harris ticket, found that of voters who ranked education as a top issue (21 percent, second only to jobs and the economy), 70 percent voted for Youngkin.

The education issue drove voter turnout. Of the voters who had not voted in 2017 but turned out in 2021, education ranked as their highest priority issue. Youngkin won this group 57 percent to 40 percent.[15]

People on both sides were left asking what happened. Who came out to vote and why?

Drawing on statistics compiled by the nonpartisan Virginia Public Access Project, Bob Brink, the chairman of the Virginia State Board of Elections, observed, "In 2021, voter turnout increased everywhere in Virginia except

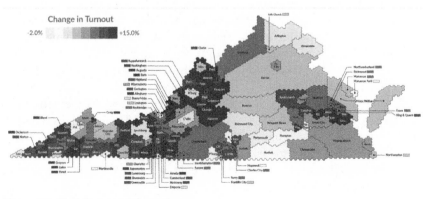

Figure 6.2. Virginia turnout by region

two relatively small jurisdictions." But the turnout was not evenly distributed. "Suburban areas like Fairfax County and Henrico County saw increases of 5 or 6 percent," he said. But in the conservative Southside and Southwest Virginia, turnout was double or triple that, with 15 percent jumps in voting turnout across the board. The Virginia Public Access Project's turnout map shows clearly where voter turnout increased the most. (See figure 6.2.)

Republican Glenn Youngkin not only won the race for governor, but he also managed to bring with him enough members of the House of Delegates to flip the chamber back to Republican control. In a post-election *Washington Post*-ABC News poll, voters were asked which party they preferred on education. Democrats still won, with 44 percent of voters choosing them. But the Republicans earned a 41 percent positive rating, higher than at any time in more than thirty years.[16]

In a state that just a year before had voted for Biden by over ten points, Youngkin won the 2021 election by 2 percent. Although turnout was predictably down from the presidential election, compared to a previous off-year election for governor, the turnout, particularly in heavily Republican areas of the state, was up. McAuliffe actually earned more votes in his losing campaign than his predecessor Ralph Northam had earned in a winning race four years earlier. But the more Republican regions of the state turned out in even higher numbers.

It was, in other words, a turnout election.

From Loudoun to Lee County, it was clear that people were certainly angry about *something.* Angry voters (not always parents, and not always district residents) began showing up at school board meetings. They also were becoming a political force.[17]

As it turned out, there were two big questions left unanswered. First, what were people so angry about? And second, did angry *parents* actually swing the election?

For right-wing pundits, post-election analysis focused largely on the narrative that parents were upset over a range of hot-button issues promoted on conservative social media. In this analysis, parents turned out to vote because they didn't want mask mandates. They wanted more control over what their kids were learning in school. And they really, really didn't want their children exposed to critical race theory.

The progressive take on the election initially focused on the notion that Democrats were worn out after four years of Donald Trump and that many of them just stayed home. That was harder to sell when turnout increased statewide. They also seemed to blame parents for falling into a CRT trap, pointing out (correctly) that CRT was not even taught in schools. But polling seemed again to dispute that explanation.

Each of these two explanations did motivate some people. But data showed that the people who were motivated by CRT were, by and large, not parents. That message appealed to hard-core partisans, and particularly to hard-core Republicans over the age of seventy-five. So CRT functioned largely as a turnout message.

To the extent that parents changed their political preferences before they went into the voting booth, it was over the issue of school closures. When early voting started in Virginia on September 17, some schools had been in session for two weeks. For parents, still reeling after nearly a year of school closures, that issue was certainly top of mind. And when they cast their ballots, they were sending a message. Plenty of parents were just fed up.

Here's what the post-election polling says and how it fits with what voters had been saying throughout the pandemic year.

WAS IT "PARENTAL RIGHTS"?

Campaigns are often defined by a single moment. Think of Michael Dukakis driving the tank or Gerald Ford saying there was no Soviet domination in Europe.

The Virginia election may well have been defined in a September 28 debate between the two candidates. It was an exchange that no one could have predicted. Republican Glenn Youngkin said to his Democratic opponent Terry McAuliffe, "You believe school systems should tell children what to do. I believe parents should be in charge of their kids' education." McAuliffe answered by saying that he was "not going to let parents come into schools and actually take books out and make their own decisions. I don't think parents should be telling schools what they should teach."[18]

Now, in fact McAuliffe had a long history of supporting parental input he could have pointed to. In his first term, he had eliminated five of the state's year-end Standards of Learning tests in elementary and middle schools, as well as the history test that had been required for graduation. That decision came over the objections of some people who were concerned that it would lead to less emphasis on the non-tested subjects, particularly science and social studies. (In the interest of full disclosure, I should note that I was one of those who expressed concerns.) At the time, McAuliffe said his decision was based on what he had had heard from parents.

He did not mention that during the debate. He did not mention it when the *Washington Post* accused him of lowering standards by eliminating the SOLs. He did not mention it later when the debate clip was turned into a Youngkin campaign ad that received heavy airplay leading up to the election, eventually putting more than $1 million behind the ad.[19]

Virginia Representative Donald McEachin criticized McAuliffe for what he called a "horrible misstatement." He added, "You cannot tell a group of people who have had, for 18 months or so, to have to home-school their children that their opinion about their children's education doesn't matter," Mr. McEachin said.[20]

CNN exit polling showed that the issue did resonate. It polled particularly well among Republican parents, with 96 percent saying that was their most resonant message.[21] But while the issue was a motivator for the Republican base, it was not what moved voters more generally. The groundwork that was laid before the 2021 Virginia election, however, did reappear later as fights over school mask mandates heated up. Voters were asked about how much parents should have a say in what schools teach. More than half—52 percent—said "a lot," and of those voters, 82 percent voted for Youngkin.[22]

CRITICAL RACE THEORY

So what about Critical Race Theory? That was the issue that certainly seemed to stroke the intellectual erogenous zones of pundits on both the right and the left. Google "CRT and Virginia election" and you'll find 850,000 results.

There's no question that race played a role in the Virginia election. Race *always* plays a role in Virginia elections. After all, Virginia is a state that enacted Massive Resistance following the Supreme Court's decision in *Brown v. Board of Education.* In 1956, Virginia voters approved the Gray Plan amendment that repealed Virginia's compulsory attendance laws, allowed the governor to close schools rather than integrate them, and provided vouchers to parents whose children enrolled in new segregated private schools.

Prince Edward County's school closures extended into the 1960s, causing US Attorney General Robert Kennedy to observe, "The only places on earth known not to provide free public education are Communist China, North Vietnam, Sarawak, Singapore, British Honduras—and Prince Edward County, Virginia."[23]

So when you're talking about race in Virginia, it's always appropriate to recall the words of William Faulkner, later quoted by Barack Obama in his speech on race in America: "The past isn't dead and buried. In fact, it isn't even past."

Certainly Manhattan Institute senior fellow Christopher F. Rufo, who is generally credited with turning CRT into a national issue, tried hard to cast the 2021 election as a referendum on CRT. "Glenn Youngkin made Critical Race Theory the closing argument to his campaign and dominated in blue Virginia," he wrote in a tweet.[24]

But in fact, as everyone from PolitiFact to Terry McAuliffe tried to say, CRT was *not* being taught in Virginia's schools. Chapter 5 highlighted the CRT debate in the suburban Loudoun County. The Standards of Learning, available to the public on the Department of Education website, could have quickly confirmed that CRT was not in the lesson plan books.

For a while, it appeared that Democrats would look at the election loss primarily through the CRT lens. Initially, pundits on the progressive left criticized not Youngkin but those who voted for him. The problem in their view was that voters were listening to what Alex Seitz-Wald, NBC's senior digital politics reporter, called "racist dog whistles from the right."[25]

On election night, Democratic pollster Cornell Belcher agreed. "Wherever you look, it looks like these college-educated, suburban white voters, who Democrats thought were breaking their way, they rallied back around Critical Race Theory."[26]

MSNBC's Nicole Wallace seemed to agree with Rufo's analysis. In a panel analyzing the Virginia results, she said, "Critical Race Theory, which isn't real, turned the suburbs fifteen points to the Trump-insurrection endorsed Republican." Former US senator Claire McCaskill and former Obama campaign manager David Plouffe nodded.[27]

Wallace wasn't wrong in suggesting CRT wasn't being taught in Virginia schools. But she was wrong in arguing that it turned the suburban vote. A deeper analysis of who voted and why showed that for many parents, CRT was not a high motivation for their vote. Remember that parents of children under the age of eighteen are no longer majority white. The thought that their children might learn about race in school was, frankly, not that frightening.

The centrist Democratic group Third Way found after reviewing the results from a number of focus groups that both parental rights and CRT "played into an existing narrative that Democrats didn't listen to parents when they kept the schools closed past any point of reason and that they'd close the schools again over parents' objections."[28]

CRT didn't cause the Democrats to lose suburbs like Loudoun. The Democratic candidate won with 55 percent of the vote. It didn't hold down turnout, which was up from 48 percent in the 2017 election to 58 percent in 2021.

What the issue did was light up Republican turnout in the far west and southwest of the state. It was particularly effective in galvanizing turnout among voters over the age of seventy-five. In those counties, which voted overwhelmingly Republican, turnout was up by 30 percent.

In a *Slate* post-election analysis, William Saletan explained why the CRT message did not appeal to parents. "That's because many parents aren't White, and the poll's nonwhite respondents were twice as likely to favor CRT as to oppose it. When Republicans talk about a parental backlash against CRT, they're not talking about all parents. They're talking about White parents."[29]

Specifically, the biggest spike in turnout was among voters over the age of seventy-five (clearly not parents of schoolchildren). A comprehensive post-election voter analysis found that turnout among this group jumped by 59 percent. Over 100,000 more seniors voted in the 2021 governor's election than voted in the any other election except the 2020 presidential election.

Those high turnout numbers that the chair of the State Board of Elections described? Almost entirely in the red areas of Virginia.

In fact, Biden/Youngkin voters said they knew that CRT was not being taught in Virginia. But at the same time, they told the focus group organizers from Third Way that "they felt like racial and social justice issues were overtaking math, history, and other things. They absolutely want their kids to hear the good and the bad of American history, at the same time they are worried that racial and cultural issues are taking over the state's curricula. . . . [The backlash] plays into another way where parents and communities feel like they are losing control over their schools in addition to the basics of even being able to decide if they're open or not."[30]

SCHOOL CLOSURES

There was a message that got some suburban parents to switch parties. Shortly after the election, Virginia political consultant Danny Barefoot led a focus group of voters who had voted for Biden in 2020 but for Youngkin in 2021. He reported on the findings on Twitter. Those participants said that, yes, they had some concerns about CRT and parental rights. But the key for them? "They felt that Democrats closed their schools and didn't feel bad about it."

That was reflected in post-election polling. The DFER/Murmuration poll found that critical race theory turned out not to have been as persuasive as concerns over school closures. While 60 percent of respondents said that keeping schools closed for in-person learning was a serious concern, fewer than half (48 percent) said the same about CRT.[31]

In addition, comments of focus group participants show how they tied some of their concerns about CRT and parental control back to school closures. As one father said, "They asked us to do all this work for months [during the time schools were closed for COVID] and then he says it's none of our business now."

In post-election analysis, Sarah Isgur and Chris Stirewalt describe the frustration that parents felt: "The public schools in Fairfax County did not open for full-time, in-person learning for the 2020–2021 school year. Not the spring after the pandemic. The whole next year. It was one of the last districts in the country to reopen even after teachers in the state got priority during the vaccine rollout. It meant a lot of parents—mostly mothers—in the state couldn't go back to work. . . . In the meantime, school boards were meeting to rename schools named after George Mason and Thomas Jefferson but not working to reopen the schools. And because it was so contrary to the science we knew at the time, a lot of folks were just angry about it."[32]

Note the juxtaposition between parents' frustration over school closures and their subsequent openness to more conservative messages. Until COVID, Fairfax County had changed the names of some schools named for Confederate heroes with a relative absence of rancor. But for many parents, changing the names of schools that were not open for instruction was infuriating.

Other questions also indicate that the issue that seemed particularly galling to parents was not the *fact* that schools had closed, but the *length* of the closure. When asked whether schools should have been closed during the COVID-19 pandemic, 65 percent said yes. But only 14 percent gave an unequivocal affirmative response, while 51 percent said that yes, schools should have closed, but they closed for too long. In addition, another 35 percent said schools should never have been closed at all. The poll found that prolonged school closures was a "resonant" message with parents (46 percent).[33]

The CEO of Murmuration, which conducted the poll referenced earlier in this chapter, reinforced this focus group message. "Frustration and stress over the continued disruption to school resulting from the pandemic, and the response from political and education leaders, is a big issue for parents," said Emma Bloomberg. She added that education "absolutely influenced voters' decisions in the recent election."[34]

That message was one I heard over and over as I talked with parents across the country. When the Drewry family chose to enroll their kids in a private school, after having moved to Fairfax County for the public schools, it was school closures that tipped the scale. "I knew that what we went through for the spring [with virtual learning at home] was not going to be good for me, for my husband, or for our kids."

Recall that in chapter 4, Democratic voters had expressed reluctance to reopening schools at the start of the 2020–2021 school year. In August of 2020, a Pew poll found that just 6 percent of Democrats or Democratic-leaning independents supported a return to full-time, in-person schooling, as compared with 36 percent of Republicans.[35]

But a year later, that had changed. By the time voters, including Democrats, had to go to the polls in 2021, school closures were on their minds. School closures, in the parlance of political consultants, was an issue that actually *moved* voters.

As Zachary Carter said in an *Atlantic* article:

> Republican Glenn Youngkin's victory in Tuesday's Virginia gubernatorial election was about schools. It wasn't about Donald Trump, or inflation, or defunding the police, or Medicare for All, or President Joe Biden's infrastructure agenda. It wasn't really about Critical Race Theory or transgender rights—though those issues shaded the situation a bit by highlighting anxieties surrounding the education system. Fundamentally, the contest was about schools—specifically, how many parents remain frustrated by the way public schools have handled the coronavirus pandemic.[36]

There were some unforced errors by the McAuliffe campaign, and they mostly played into the anger over school closures. During the days just before the election, when candidates typically barnstorm across the state accompanied by luminaries who will help them draw a crowd, Terry McAuliffe chose to campaign with American Federation of Teachers president Randi Weingarten.

The choice was puzzling in several ways: first, because Virginia's teachers overwhelmingly belong to the National Education Association, she did not have a natural constituency. Second, parents were well aware of Weingarten's "nothing is off the table" comments regarding keeping schools closed in 2020. In one of the post-election focus groups, a parent articulated her anger at seeing Weingarten with McAuliffe. "They [the teacher's union] would keep schools closed forever if they could. They'd keep our kids online until the 7th booster."[37]

Over the long haul, it will be problematic for Democrats if parents begin to link "teachers," whom they generally like and respect, with "teachers unions." There was at least a whiff of that in the DFER/Murmuration poll, with many Biden/Youngkin voters suggesting that the prolonged school closures were based on what unions wanted rather than on science. For candidates who have happily pasted "Teacher Endorsed" stickers on their campaign signs, that issue is one that bears watching.

National Parents Union president Keri Rodriguez summed it up. "Folks like me have been saying for the past 18 months, you are underestimating the level of anxiety, fear and frankly, the erosion of the relationship that schools have come to rely on when it comes to parents and families right now," she said.[38]

A *Politico* postelection analysis quoted Republican strategist Rory Cooper, who lives in Northern Virginia. "If they opened up the schools in the fall of 2020, Terry McAuliffe wins. Democrats always have underestimated how many *Democrats* were mad at the school closures."[39]

SAN FRANCISCO RECALL ELECTION

In San Francisco, where schools were closed longer than nearly anywhere else in the nation, parents began to focus more on their local school board meetings. There were many serious issues for the board to discuss. The district, which served more than fifty thousand students at the start of the pandemic, was facing both declining enrollment and a growing budget deficit. The superintendent, Vincent Matthews, had announced his resignation, so the board also needed to address hiring his replacement.

There was very little controversy about school closures during the spring of 2020. It's fair to say that people in San Francisco take public health issues very seriously. The city's gay population was decimated by AIDS. The city's Asian population had been particularly careful following SARS. There was no vaccine, and the state of California had adopted stringent measures to slow the spread of the virus.

Over the summer, however, parents began to wonder when schools might reopen. They began tuning in to watch school board meetings. Schools around the country began reopening. Then schools within the state of California began in-person learning. The city's private schools announced they would bring students back to their classrooms.

Spencer Potter's frustration was similar to that of many San Francisco parents. "What I really want the schools to appreciate and acknowledge is the dual role that they play. The school board only thinks of themselves as an educating entity and not a childcare entity. But our whole work-life structure is premised on the fact that schools also care for our kids. That's part of the public trust that we place in schools."

When parents were home and online anyway, they began to tune in—literally—to how the district was governed. That led them to watch the meetings of the San Francisco school board. The 2020–2021 school year dragged on, with no reopening plans in sight. And that was when the frustration began to boil over.

Two of those parents were Autumn Looijen and her partner Siva Raj, two tech industry professionals. Neither had never been involved with politics. Looijen was the parent of three children in the Los Altos school district, one of the first to reopen. Her children were happy and learning. But Raj's sons were in the San Francisco Unified School District schools, still fully remote. His teenager was disengaged, silent, and failing his online classes.

Plans for reopening were not what Looijen and Raj heard when they watched school board meetings. The typical board meeting, they told Ryan Lizza on the *Playbook Deep Dive* podcast, lasted seven hours. "And school reopening was always the last thing on the agenda. It felt like they didn't care about the one thing they should have cared about. "[40]

What was the board discussing instead? One meeting involved a lengthy discussion of an appointment to the board's Parent Advisory Board. At the time, there were five vacancies on the board. A majority of the board members were persons of color, and all of them were women. One of the candidates was a gay teacher who was the father of biracial children.

After a two-hour discussion, board members blocked the appointment because it would temporarily have tipped the composition of the board to majority white. (There was no discussion of filling another of the vacancies with a person of color, thus tipping the board majority back.) That meant that there were no LGBTQ members on the Parent Advisory Board in San Francisco.

Adding to families' frustration was the school board's decision to rename forty-four district schools that the board alleged had been linked to racism or oppression.

The issue spiraled when it became clear that the reasons given for some of the school renamings were based on research that was inadequate at best. There were no historians on the group that came up with the ratings, but Wikipedia was cited as a source for renaming seven of the schools.[41] (Parents were curious why schools named for Dianne Feinstein, Paul Revere, and Abraham Lincoln, for example, were slated to be renamed.) The move seemed particularly tone deaf in view of the fact that the district's families were far more concerned about getting their children back into classrooms, whatever the school might be called.

"They [the school board] were really focused on racial justice," Raj said. They prioritized addressing "the symbols of inequity—changing the names above the door. They see these things as tools of a society that has been deeply unfair to a lot of people. But they didn't want to do the hard work of actually fixing educational outcomes for our kids."[42]

The proposal, and its timing, brought the city together, with progressives and conservatives both harshly critical. San Francisco Mayor London Breed issued a statement highlighting the source of families' unhappiness:[43]

> What I cannot understand is why the School Board is advancing a plan to have all these schools renamed by April, when there isn't a plan to have our kids back in the classroom by then. Our students are suffering, and we should be talking about getting them in classrooms, getting them mental health support, and getting them the resources they need in this challenging time. Our families are frustrated about a lack of a plan, and they are especially frustrated with the fact that the discussion[s] of these plans weren't even on the agenda for last night's School Board meeting.

The board eventually withdrew the motion to rename the schools. But by then, families were even more upset with a school board that seemed not to be listening to their concerns.

In mid-April, after most school districts in the state had started bringing students back into the classroom, the district announced a phased return to in-person learning. The announcement included many qualifiers and was actually silent about when middle and high school students would return. SFUSD did note that in-person schooling for priority populations (newcomer students, students demonstrating limited online engagement, homeless students, foster youth, students in public housing, and Special Day Class students in grades 6–13) would resume by April 29.[44]

On April 7, the district announced its commitment to providing students "the option to return to full-time in-person school." The guarantee, however, would not take effect until "the first day of the 2021–2022 academic school year, assuming public health guidelines allow."[45]

The third issue that motivated parents was a change in the admission policies to the district's prestigious Lowell High School. At the time, Lowell's student body was 51 percent Asian American, 18 percent white, 11.5 percent Hispanic, and 2 percent Black.[46] Board members were concerned about the lack of representation for Black and Latino students.

Until the pandemic closed schools, Lowell's admissions process had used a combination of GPA and state testing scores to determine who would be admitted. But in view of school closures, the board decided to temporarily change to a random lottery. That temporary change became permanent in February of 2021.

The issue particularly resonated in the Asian community. "Lowell has been a place where immigrant families could come to the city with no money and no connections," Raj said. "Their kids spend their entire childhoods working to pass this exam so they can go to Lowell and have a better life."

Using all volunteers and pledging to accept no contribution larger than $99, the Recall the School Board organization (RecallSFSchoolBoard.org) started the effort to recall three members of the school board in February 2021 (the other four were elected so recently that they were not eligible for recall). They needed to gather 51,325 valid signatures to get the issue on the ballot. By September, they had exceeded their goal and the recall measures were authorized to go on the ballot.

Recall elections are expensive and generally unsuccessful. But the message was compelling: Pay attention to making sure that the actual work of your job is done. "If you're not reading well at the end of third grade, your chances of dropping out of school skyrocket. We couldn't wait. So to school board members, if you want to rename 44 schools, please make sure that the kids inside those walls can read."

By the fall of the 2021–2022 school year, enrollment in the district had dropped by 6.6 percent, or roughly 3,500 students. The district estimated that decline would lead to a loss of about $35 million in state funding.[47] That led to further concerns that the school board was not focused on the most important issues.

The election campaign was hard fought and occasionally bitter, but on February 15, 2022, the results were overwhelming. Roughly 75 percent of voters cast ballots to recall the three board members, Alison Collins, Gabriela López, and Faauuga Moliga. That represented more voters than had elected them in the first place. On election day, turnout by Chinese Americans was 50 percent higher than usual. The precinct surrounding Lowell High School had the highest vote total in favor of the recall of any precinct in the city, with over 90 percent supporting.

"From day one, the campaign was a campaign to get politics out of education," Raj said. "What we saw consistently was a pattern where the school board leadership focused on a lot of political stunts and symbolic gestures like trying to rename schools, and doing that ultimately badly."[48]

Perhaps the San Francisco school board recall will be a political unicorn— a one-time event that is not replicated anywhere else. But when people become politically active, they often remain involved.

Once people have gotten involved with politics, said David Campbell, a professor at Notre Dame University in the *Christian Science Monitor*, "it often spills over and they will be engaged in other forms of political activity." The debate surrounding school segregation in the 1950s primed many Americans for broader activism in the 1960s.

"This is not the first time we have seen issues around public schools be flash points for controversy," Campbell said. "You can think of school board politics as the gateway drug to greater involvement across the board."[49]

OTHER SCHOOL BOARD RECALL ELECTIONS

The San Francisco board recalls were among the most highly publicized in the country. But they did not represent the only places where vocal groups tried to remove school board members from office.

Efforts to recall school board members spiked in 2021, according to the website Ballotpedia. The site recorded ninety-two recall efforts in 2021, compared with a typical number of about thirty per year. Of the ninety-two elections, one board member was recalled.[50]

In Ozaukee County's Mequon-Thiensville School District in the suburbs north of Milwaukee, a recall election targeted four school board members. The high-profile race attracted large out-of-district contributions and national publicity. But in the end, all four incumbents were reelected with an average vote of 58 percent.[51] The *Milwaukee Sentinel Journal* reported the election was the sixteenth unsuccessful school board recall election in Wisconsin.

In Kenosha, Wisconsin, three school board members survived a recall attempt. However, the county's electors (essentially a town meeting) then voted to slash their salaries from $6,500 per year to $100 per meeting. The $100 would be paid only if the board member attended the meeting in person.[52]

There is no question that local school board elections are becoming more nationalized. In April school board elections in Wisconsin, the trend continued. Waukesha County, which voted for Donald Trump in 2020, elected conservatives to the local school board. But in other blue and purple areas, including Oshkosh, Fond du Lac, Eau Claire, and LaCrosse, more moderate or progressive school board candidates were successful.

Increasingly, people see themselves as members of one party or the other, and they view everything through that lens. State legislative races now frequently include discussions of national issues. Since education is currently an issue that is top of mind for voters, it's to be expected that local school board races will be politicized.

The most effective way to recall any elected official, of course, is to defeat them at the polls in a general election. It will be harder to track the number of board members who resign rather than face a vitriolic reelection campaign or are defeated in their next election. One of the organizers of the Mequon-Thiensville School District recall, for example, is now running as a candidate in a regular school board election.

Again, that's not new. Chapter 5 described how the nonpartisan elections in Fairfax County were politicized as early as 1995. But then, even as voters were asked to vote on the national issue of whether creationism should be taught in Fairfax County science classes, they were also focused on a number of local issues.

The county had a desperate need for more schools and classrooms, and how we were going to manage that growth was a big issue. The election also took place during a time of enormous demographic change in the county. A growing number of students were entering school speaking a language that was not English. The challenge for the school system was to meet every student's needs while also ensuring that student achievement levels remained high. Those were conversations that were held at voter forums throughout the campaign.

We were fortunate in that race, and in our subsequent term as elected school board members, to have the coverage of superb education reporters, including some like Peter Baker, now the chief White House correspondent for the *New York Times*, and Robert O'Harrow, now an investigative reporter for the *Washington Post.* They provided in-depth reporting on issues like school boundary changes and school budgets. While as the subject of their coverage I sometimes wished they were a little less driven by the pursuit of the story, I know they worked hard to give an accurate portrayal of the school system.

But in many communities, according to Vladimir Kogan, associate professor of political science at Ohio State University, the hollowing out of local newspapers means that there are often school board meetings with no reporters present. That means that community members often have no way to keep abreast of local-specific issues.

"Historically, local news was a primary source of information about education," he said. "As local newspapers were taken over by private equity firms, and as local television stations are bought by organizations like Sinclair Media, local news reporters are often the first to be laid off in a cost-cutting measure." That has led to an erosion of outlets to cover local news and in turn a much greater reliance, even in these supposedly local news outlets, on national news stories.

So now when voters are looking for information on which candidate to vote for, there will be a much heavier emphasis on national news. While parents will still have access to other information about their child's school—through school newsletters or emails from the school district—nonparents will not. That also may help explain the number of Virginia voters ages seventy-five and older who voted on education issues that did not reflect what was going on in schools.

Local news outlets are important. As William McKinzie wrote in *The Catalyst,* a publication of the George W. Bush Institute, "[A] local source of news helps create a shared culture. We live in a time when all sorts of political, social, and public health issues are tearing away at our notion of community. A respected news operation becomes a place to air grievances, discuss problems, learn about neighbors, celebrate big moments, and define the identity of the community. Not perfectly, but it is a way to strengthen the bonds of community."[53]

Given the absence of local news outlets in many communities, it is even more important for schools to devote time and energy to talking and listening to their communities. It is unquestionably a time-intensive process. But it's also a little bit like the old commercial that said, "You can pay me now or you can pay me later." Schools can communicate early, or they can wait for crowds of angry (and possibly misinformed) citizens to show up at the next school board meeting.

If parents want school board members who reflect their interests, they need to do the hard work of organizing campaigns. As the San Francisco recall parents discovered, it's hard and exacting and not always the most exciting work in the world. But parents can be mobilized, and they can ensure that their local boards reflect the majority and not just a small but vocal minority.

Education has historically been an issue that brings people together, and it still can be. The San Francisco school board election recall actually creates a blueprint for a successful campaign. The organizers focused on a simple message: focus on what you were elected to do. As Mayor London Breed said, the voters expect the school board to spend their time on the "essentials of delivering a well-run school system above all else."

Second, do the hard work of voter contact. The San Francisco organizers were in every neighborhood. Unsurprisingly for a campaign created by two tech professionals, the San Francisco effort relied on technology to spread their message. The Chinese-language messaging app WeChat helped spread the word about how to fill out a ballot and coordinated schedules for volunteers who used lion dances and drumming as part of their Get Out the Vote effort.

The San Francisco campaign organizers took particular pride in the widespread support they found among all the city's racial and ethnic communities. "If we can bring together everyone on this issue—Republicans to Berniecrats to Green Party members—everyone can agree that kids deserve a good education. As divided as we are, we can still agree on that."

LONG-TERM POLITICAL THREATS
TO PUBLIC SCHOOLS

One of the consequences of the extended school closures may be a more existential threat to public education. In several states, governors and legislators stepped in to support parents who were angry that their children were out of school.

Arizona governor Doug Ducey announced that he would use federal American Rescue Plan Act funding to provide vouchers to families whose children's schools were closed or moved to remote learning. The Open for Learning Recovery Benefit program would fund up to $7,000 for approved child care or school tuition related to school closures. Applicants can earn up to 350 percent of the federal poverty level—$92,750 for a family of four. The program would be available "if schools close for even one day," the governor said in announcing the program.[54] Governor Ducey is a long-time supporter of school choice programs, and the program he announced was on shaky ground since the US Treasury Department had already issued warnings that two similar programs would not qualify for American Rescue Plan Act funding.

Still, the Arizona proposal reflected a more general recognition on the part of voucher proponents that parents' frustration with school closures might persuade some formerly staunch public school advocates to at least reconsider their position.

The National Conference of State Legislatures noted in April of 2021 that "legislatures in at least 37 states are considering bills that would expand or introduce private school choice programs." Bills in Georgia, Kansas, Louisiana, and New Hampshire introduced new Education Savings Accounts (ESAs) designed specifically to respond to parents' frustration with online instruction. ESAs, unlike school vouchers, provide state funding that families may use for a range of educational expenses, including not only private school tuition (available through voucher programs) but also curriculum, technology, and assessments associated with home education.[55]

Michael Bloomberg announced that his philanthropic organization would donate $750 million to create 150,000 seats in charter schools. "American public education is broken," he wrote in a *Wall Street Journal* opinion essay. "Since the pandemic began, students have experienced severe learning loss because schools remained closed in 2020—and even in 2021 when vaccinations were available to teachers and it was clear schools could reopen safely. Many schools also failed to administer remote learning adequately."[56]

One could disagree with his solution. But it was hard to argue with his assessment of remote learning.

CHAPTER 7

UNFINISHED LEARNING

> There is only one thing more painful than learning from experience, and that is not learning from experience.
>
> —Archibald MacLeish

"Start planning for the next forced school closure. It will come. And next time, schools and districts will need to act quickly, not dither for months." Those words from Robin Lake, director of the Center on Reinventing Public Education, are an ominous portent of what is very likely to happen again.

In fact, school closures are continuing even as this chapter is being written, some two years after the first pandemic closure. In the first week of January 2022, according to the website Burbio, an estimated 5,225 schools in the United States were closed or doing virtual learning at least one day. Some closures were caused by snowstorms. In at least one large district (Chicago), the schools were closed because of an ongoing failure of the school district and the teachers union to agree on COVID safety procedures.

The largest cause of school closures remains COVID, but most are not due to widespread transmission among students. They're due to a lack of substitute teachers. "Increasingly, we are seeing that it's a lack of staff that causes schools to shut down," says Dan Domenech of AASA. "That is likely to continue."

And that will continue to be a problem. In January 2022, poll expert Nate Silver of FiveThirtyEight tweeted: Why are Democratic politicians acting like school closures are a huge political liability? Well, because they are. Shifting schools to remote learning is opposed 30–66 in the latest Suffolk/USA Today poll. Even a majority of Democrats (52 percent) oppose.[1] (Interestingly, and perhaps related, when respondents to that Suffolk poll were asked to sum up the year 2021 in one word, the leading response by far was "Awful/Terrible/Bad/Sucked.")[2]

There are lessons to be learned. Even before the pandemic, there were models of how to "do" school in a new way. During the pandemic, they were stress tested and proved to be successful in helping navigate through those challenging times.

Now these models can, and should, be more widely available. Here are some of the most important lessons that can be learned from the pandemic:

LESSON #1: ACKNOWLEDGE THE REALITY OF LEARNING LOSS

As school closures lingered (and lingered), there was a curious and frustrating change in nomenclature. Initially, there was much discussion about how to deal with learning loss. Which was, of course, accurate. Children had lost ground in their education, and the longer the pandemic lingered, the more acute the problem seemed to be.

But in the spring of 2021, there was a concerted effort to change the language. Instead of learning *loss*, we were to talk about "unfinished learning." Or, even more frustrating, we were supposed to deny that there was any loss at all.

In some quarters, there was what felt like a coordinated effort to act as though in-person school didn't matter. In August, *Los Angeles Magazine* profiled Cecily Myart-Cruz, head of that city's teachers union. "There is no such thing as learning loss," she said when she was asked how school closures might have affected the nearly six hundred thousand students in the school district. "Our kids didn't lose anything. It's OK that our babies may not have learned all their times tables. They learned resilience. They learned survival. They learned critical-thinking skills. They know the difference between a riot and a protest. They know the words *insurrection* and *coup*."[3]

For parents who were themselves working on the front lines in hospitals or fire stations or grocery stores, statements like that were infuriating. Parents know their kids are struggling. Teachers know kids are behind.

We have been here before. During the Carter administration, when America was in a recession, economist Alfred Kahn headed up the administration's task force on the recession. There was just one problem: he was told he couldn't say the word *recession*. So Kahn took to substituting the word *banana*. As in, "Between 1973 and 1975, we had the deepest banana that we had in 35 years, and yet inflation dipped only very briefly."[4]

A more honest, and likely more effective, approach came from the Newark, New Jersey, Teachers Union. In March of 2022, they used learning loss as a challenge when the results of midyear state exams came in showing dismal results (2 percent of fourth graders were projected to be on grade level by the end of the year). The teacher group said, in essence, yes, there's learning loss. There's a lot of learning loss. And schools can't address the problem by themselves. "Where is the sense of urgency with learning loss?" asked John Abeigon, president of the union. He called for a community-wide effort to address the issue. "Acknowledge that it exists, sit down as a group, and let's see how we're going to tackle this."[5]

Here's the reality: you cannot solve a problem if you do not acknowledge it. Simply changing the nomenclature did nothing to address the very real challenges that students faced after more than a year in virtual learning. The Scarlett O'Hara "I'll just think about that tomorrow" approach just flat doesn't work.

Alternatively, we can all agree just to call it a banana.

LESSON #2: PERMANENTLY CLOSE
THE DIGITAL DIVIDE

If there were any positive outcomes to COVID school closures, one would have to be the influx of funding that helped close the digital divide. Within a year, many districts were able to provide computers or tablets to every student.

Even with the new funding, there are still too many families without access to the high-speed internet that makes online learning possible. Connectivity is not a one-and-done proposition: estimates are that there will be a permanent cost of between $280 and $500 per student to keep students connected.[6]

The E-rate and Lifeline programs provide durable funding to ensure schools, communities, and low-income households continue to be able to access essential communications technology. State initiatives also show some promise. Working with local school districts and community organizations, they should create long-term plans to ensure everyone has access to high-speed internet.

Schools and districts need to continue striving toward full digital inclusion for every student. As the National Digital Inclusion Alliance defines the term, it means "activities necessary to ensure that all individuals and communities, including the most disadvantaged, have access to and use of information and communication technologies." NDIA includes five key elements:

- Affordable and robust high-speed internet
- Internet-enabled devices that meet users' needs
- Access to digital literacy training for students and parents
- Quality technical support
- Applications and online content designed to enable and encourage self-sufficiency, participation, and collaboration.[7]

The second step will be a clear-eyed evaluation of what worked, and what didn't when school went online. This book includes many stories of families that tried hard to keep their children engaged in virtual learning. Most of them were frustrated and felt the system just didn't work for their kids.

Teachers are not to blame, but they are a key part of any solution. Just as teacher education programs in the not-too-distant past required teachers to learn about bulletin boards, now preservice educators need to learn how to plan and conduct engaging lessons online.

They also need access to the best lesson plans and curriculum resources so they don't have to create everything from the ground up. Well before the pandemic, Louisiana's Department of Education was providing reviews of high-quality resources and professional development to guide instruction, some of which are available for free online. In addition, organizations like Open Up Resources and UnboundEd provide free, high-quality comprehensive curricula for mathematics and English language arts on their websites.

Third, teachers need support in making technology a part of their in-person education. Mostly, that didn't happen post-pandemic. In part that may have been because both teachers and students were very happy to be communicating in person and not through a screen. But it's possible to maintain some of the strengths of digital learning even while students are in a physical classroom.

For example, as parent Kara Stup pointed out in chapter 4, some of the technology tools used during virtual learning helped not only students with autism, but every student in the class. Even when students are learning in person, the teacher could ask a question of the entire class and have students use a class management software program to monitor students' screens.

That way, every student, not just the one or two who raised their hand, would have to be engaged with the question. Without having to walk around the classroom and look at every student's paper, the teacher would also be aware of whether students had understood the lesson and were paying attention or not. And for students with autism, who need both time and quiet to process their thoughts, this approach would allow them to do their best in class.

Some students will want or need to continue with virtual instruction. They may have health issues that make it difficult to be in close contact with other students. They may simply prefer to have time to pursue other interests. (Many elite gymnasts and ice skaters spend at least part of their middle and high school years learning online.)

However, virtual learning will have to up its game. A good virtual school will not be exactly like a good in-person school. Class times are likely to be shorter. (Spending forty-five minutes or an hour staring at a screen is, as anyone who lived through a Zoom meeting knows, a challenge.)

There may also be parents who want to combine in-school learning with scheduled time at home. While current school schedules make that a herculean task, it is worth exploring in the future. This type of schedule would also make it easier for students to participate in work-study or internship opportunities.

LESSON #3: WHEN SCHOOLS CLOSE, PARENTS SHOULDN'T HAVE TO GO IT ALONE

Nearly every parent interviewed for this book talked about the tremendous feeling of isolation they experienced when they were trying to combine work, childcare, and school.

For parents of children with disabilities, the pandemic school closures proved especially isolating. Parents in this book shared the sacrifices they made to keep their kids from a complete educational meltdown. They quit jobs. They sat with their student and functioned as an instructional assistant full time.

That is not sustainable in the long run. But schools can look for better ways to engage students in online learning. A greater use of breakout rooms or one-on-one conversations with instructional aides or learning coaches would be one way to help.

One other possible solution would be to use technology to create more, but shorter, IEP meetings. One COVID experiment allowed parents and school staff to meet biweekly to discuss educational progress and to make quick adjustments.[8]

In some families, grandparents stepped in and provided sessions on FaceTime or Zoom to stay connected with their grandchildren. They read books together. They helped with homework. They listened to their grandchildren practice a musical instrument. They built a stronger bond and also helped their grandchildren in school.

Communities and nonprofit organizations should also work with schools to use technology to link students with family members or older mentors who can connect virtually. In Austin, Texas, students from the University of Texas at Austin created an online platform to link the generations. Big & Mini (bigandmini.org) is, according to its website, "our best effort at using technology to shrink the generational divide into a small crack."

Interested volunteers must complete a training program before they are matched with a student. At the arranged time, both call into the organization's phone platform and carry on their conversation. There is a mobile app and a one-tap option for volunteers who may not be particularly tech-savvy.

Another organization that matches students with older volunteers is Eldera (eldera.ai). Volunteers must all have "six decades or more of life experience," as the organization's website explains it. They need a computer with an internet connected to Zoom. They must be willing to pass a background check "for parents' peace of mind and for everyone's safety."

The organization matches mentors and mentees based on similar interests. They typically meet once a week for thirty to sixty minutes. Parents are required to be present for the first meeting but not for subsequent meetings.

Neither of these organizations is a tutoring program. Rather, they create the same kind of one-on-one relationship that a grandparent might have with a grandchild.

LESSON #4: USE RESEARCH-BASED TUTORING TO CLOSE LEARNING GAPS

Research showed that tutoring was one of the most promising ways to address the learning gap. As the late Robert Slavin from Johns Hopkins University, probably the nation's foremost expert on tutoring to close learning gaps, wrote:

> It has long been known that tutoring is the most effective strategy for accelerating the learning of students struggling in reading and math. Every educator knows this, of course, because when their own children are struggling in school, they get them a tutor. The research just provides evidence to back up common sense. Not all tutoring is effective; it does matter how you do it, which is why it is essential that educators use proven approaches. But "tutoring works" is not big news.[9]

The problem, of course, is that tutoring at the ratio that research shows is most effective (generally a group size of 4 or fewer) is expensive. But when the federal COVID relief money started pouring in to schools, launching a tutoring program was suddenly affordable.

Schools, nonprofit organizations, and then, inevitably, for-profit organizations suddenly lined up to provide tutoring for students. The offerings were, well, uneven.

We know what works. During the pandemic, I helped establish a new nonprofit organization, known as EduTutorVA, that drew heavily on Robert Slavin's work at Johns Hopkins University. It combined these elements:

- Small tutor-to-student ratio (two or three students). Research told us that groups of two or three were most effective in addressing learning loss.

Interestingly, for English-language learners small group sessions were more effective

- Frequent contact. We scheduled a research-based two or three tutoring sessions per week, each one lasting between thirty and forty-five minutes for younger students and up to an hour for older students.
- Trained tutors. Our partnership with George Mason University and Northern Virginia Community College gave us access to aspiring educators. Our goal of strengthening the tutor-to-teacher pipeline turned out to be a unique feature of EduTutorVA. Our conversations with educators confirmed that far too often, teachers are unprepared to deal with diverse students who are performing below grade level. We gave aspiring educators practical experience so they could begin their teaching careers with skills in diagnosing and addressing these students' learning needs.
- Regular diagnostic testing. A partnership with NWEA allowed us to give students the Map Growth assessment. This accomplished two goals: first, it gave tutors specific information about where to pinpoint their instruction. If a student is two years behind, it makes no sense to reteach something the student already knows. Second, it gave our aspiring educators a familiarity with using data to support instruction.

Tutoring can and does work. But if tutors are not trained, if they are not committed to meeting regularly with students, and if they are not able to diagnose students' learning problems, the tutoring will not be as effective as it could be. If schools try to save money by piling large groups into tutoring sessions, they should not be surprised if they don't get good results. Following the research is the key to helping students succeed.

Although there was a rush to provide in-person tutoring once schools reopened, the EduTutorVA experience is that virtual tutoring can sometimes be preferrable. We had started virtually, but originally thought that we might move to in-person tutoring once schools reopened. However, we have learned that this model provides many benefits, including flexible scheduling and more time for tutors to teach.

One of our tutors, a disabled veteran, likely could not manage the logistics of traveling across the county to two schools in Mount Vernon. But with a virtual platform, she was able to connect easily with students. As a wounded vet whose own parents were often deployed in the military, she has been a particularly effective tutor working with other students whose parents have also been deployed. That personal relationship adds to her instructional strengths.

LESSON #5: CHANGE THE ONE-TEACHER-
ONE-CLASSROOM MODEL

The idea that one teacher could spend all day in a classroom with twenty-five to thirty students, meeting all their needs in every subject, was frankly already unsustainable long before 2020. Students increasingly arrive in school with wide disparities in what they know and what they need. Teachers were frustrated and stressed by their inability to address all those needs, no matter how hard they worked.

"Then schools closed," said Carole Basile, dean and professor at the Mary Lou Fulton Teachers College at Arizona State University (MLFTC). "What we said to teachers was, 'Not only are we asking you to be all things to all kids. Now we are asking you to be all things to all kids . . . remotely.'"

Experience showed that it didn't work, because it couldn't. Even when teaching hours were reduced, teachers were spending long hours trying to create lesson plans. The RAND American Teacher Panel found that teachers were spending as much as thirty hours each week on lesson planning, and that more teachers were devoting more hours teaching and planning than they had before the pandemic.

Even as teachers reported working longer and harder than ever, they knew students weren't learning. But they reached a point where they couldn't do anything more by themselves. Teachers needed support from other teachers. They needed flexibility. And they needed the time to personalize learning for their students. All that, says Dan Domenech, the executive director of AASA, meant that "the traditional notion of one teacher in a classroom with twenty-five kids for all day is no longer going to work."

And things didn't improve over time. In January of 2021, CRPE reviewed the available teacher surveys to see how teachers were faring nine months into the pandemic. They learned:

- Teachers' workloads spiked in the spring of 2020 and really never let up.
- All teachers, but especially those teaching remotely and in high-poverty schools, struggled to provide instruction, engage students, and manage technology.
- Morale had fallen sharply and seemed to be getting worse as challenges built.

It is not surprising that people are less interested in becoming teachers. Fewer and fewer people are entering the teaching profession. Between 2011 and 2016, there was a 35 percent decline in the number of people enrolled in a teacher education program, according to US Department of Education data reported by Arizona State University.[10] "We continue to look at the problem as a recruitment-retention problem," Basile points out. "But in fact, it's a workforce development problem."

MLFTC is working on a new model of school staffing that could provide teachers with more support and flexibility while also improving student learning. The SPARK School in the Kyrene school district in Tempe, Arizona, offers a window into what this new way of organizing schools might look like.

Early in the 2019–2020 school year, and before the pandemic hit, the school district created the SPARK School pilot. (The name is an acronym for Student-led, Project-based, Achieving, Real-world, Knowledge.) Teachers worked in multigrade teams. The first-year pilot at SPARK included teams of one full-time teacher leader, two other certified teachers, and three teaching residents from MLFTC. Community educators offered special classes like yoga. The local state senator taught students how to draft a bill to support endangered animal species.

Students met in "learning studios" and focused on project-based learning activities. Multiage grouping meant that student learning was personalized so students were achieving curriculum standards whether they were above, on, or below grade level. Students moved through the learning studio and teachers regularly reconfigured learning spaces. A typical day would include small-group instruction, collaborative hands-on learning, one-on-one teaching, as well as full-class discussions. Technology was a big part of the school day, and students were encouraged to develop a familiarity with online learning platforms like Google Classroom.

By midyear, teachers decided also to borrow some techniques from flipped classroom models. Specifically, they tried to prerecord direct instruction to help students develop playlists of instructional activities.

Basically, playlists are like road maps—they lay out a series of lessons, outline assignments they must complete, and then culminate in a final assessment. That is very much like a traditional unit lesson plan, except that with a playlist, *students* are responsible for working through the playlist. They know what they have accomplished and what they have yet to complete. Each student's playlist can be customized to meet their individual needs.[11]

By the time schools closed for the pandemic, educators were comfortable in planning individualized instruction. And students already had the tech skills that allowed them to get online and start working. All that made the transition to virtual learning "less of a stretch," according to MLFTC.[12]

Over the summer, SPARK School educators offered some learning activities to keep kids engaged. They did remote read-alouds, tutoring sessions, and even social events.

When in-person learning resumed, the class day still combined some online learning with in-person instruction for students who chose to be in school. Zoom breakout rooms allowed small groups of students to meet whether they were at their home or in the classroom. Students continued to work on personalized playlists they help develop.

This staffing approach allows teachers to support each other. If a student needs individual help, a staff member can provide it immediately. When students need special education services, they can get them as part of their regular schooling. Approaches like this will make better use of teacher professionalism and also help students by personalizing learning.

Teachers also need clear recommendations on curriculum materials and lesson plans. Some states and school systems are doing an excellent job of providing suggestions for high-quality curriculum materials and resources. For example, even before the pandemic, Louisiana's Department of Education was providing reviews of high-quality resources and professional development to guide instruction, some of which are available for free online. In addition, organizations like Open Up Resources and UnboundEd provide free, high-quality comprehensive curricula for mathematics and English language arts on their websites.

LESSON # 6: OPEN UP EDUCATION POLICY MAKING

Local school board elections used to be sleepy affairs. They were rarely held at the same time as an election for president or Congress. Most candidates raised a few hundred dollars, perhaps enough to put up a few signs in the yards of supporters. On the night before the election, people would call a PTA activist they knew and ask, "Who am I supposed to vote for?"

These races have been low-turnout, low-information events. According to the National School Boards Association (NSBA), voter turnout is often "discouragingly low"—often just 5 or 10 percent. NSBA offers several examples:

- Only 8.7 percent of eligible Los Angeles County voters participated in the 2019 local school board election;
- In a school district in Iowa, 498 voters—10.05 percent of registered voters—decided the 2017 race for school board members;
- In South Dakota, in a school district with 2,054 voters at the time of the election, only 245 (12 percent) participated in the local school board election.[13]

Now that education politics is the grist for a particular brand of nationalized anger messaging, school board elections will no longer be sedate and polite. We're looking at bare-knuckle politics for the foreseeable future.

That is not an accident. According to Christopher F. Rufo, an activist and a senior fellow at the Manhattan Institute who launched a crusade against CRT, the goal from the start was to use the issue to drive voters to the polls. "We are building the most sophisticated political movement in America—and we have just begun," he wrote on Twitter on November 2, the night of the Virginia election.[14]

In reflecting on the 2022 Wisconsin school board races, State Democratic Chair Ben Wickler tweeted, "If the spring is predictive of the fall—and honestly, it's never a straight line from one to the other—then the most valid takeaway is this: Wisconsin is going to be intense, turnout will be huge, and both sides will have to fight for every vote."[15]

Local school boards are hardly perfect. But Americans still want education policy set at the local level. That means that local school boards and local school districts will need to be more active in their communications and outreach efforts.

In April 2022, the Loudoun County School Board created a new parent advisory committee. The Loudoun Education Alliance of Families (LEAF) is "an advisory group voice for parents to elevate educational concerns and provide feedback to the board on current or proposed policies or issues facing the school board." Each school's parent-teacher organization can nominate one individual to serve on the council, with the school board making final decisions. The charter of the organization specifies that members must be parents of a student in the school system.

The motion creating LEAF highlights the importance of two-way communication between parents and schools. "Parents have a unique understanding of their children's experiences and can offer insights about proposed policies, strategies and educational needs. Members of LEAF will share School Board information back to their respective communities, becoming a two-way conduit for information, helping improve student experience."[16]

This type of council could provide a better way to share information about the county schools with a group representing parent leaders from across the county. Many districts have some sort of parent advisory council, but having elected members and monthly meetings can strengthen their role.

On the other hand, school boards may want to look at their policies on public comments at local school board meetings. Communicating with the school board does offer citizens First Amendment protections. This means the public generally has the right to speak regarding matters within the jurisdiction of the school board. The board, however, may place reasonable restrictions as to the time, place, and manner of the speech. Boards can prohibit someone from repeating the same comments at multiple meetings or limit the amount of time for public comment at the meeting as a whole. Any such policies, however, must be consistently enforced on a content-neutral basis.

It is not unreasonable to expect that the only people allowed to address the board should be residents of the area served by the board. It is not unreasonable to ask that speakers address only issues that are on the agenda for a particular meeting. If a school board has the authority to hire and fire the superintendent and perhaps a few senior administrators, then it can reasonably prohibit a citizen who wants to complain about the conduct of a particular teacher or coach from testifying, for example.[17]

It may also be worthwhile to set aside a speaking slot or two for students. In many cases, some of the most mature reactions to adult behavior at school board meetings have come from students. In Douglas County, Nevada, senior Jacob Lewis suggested that adults should consider the impact their words can have on students. "We should be listening to each other instead of fighting and understanding how the other person thinks. And more importantly why they think that way and listening to their argument. Those adults are supposed to be our role models."[18]

EPILOGUE

When the 2021–2022 school year started, the families I spoke with were starting to return to something that felt like "normal." But nearly all of them believe that COVID school closures have had an impact on their children.

Elena Guarinello and Jessica Latterman's daughter returned to in-person learning as soon as Montgomery County offered them the option. "When we had a choice about sending her back to in-person learning, we said, 'Yes, please,'" Elena said. Now in a program that provides enriched learning, their daughter does have a few knowledge gaps of things she might ordinarily have learned in third grade. "I don't think she lost anything, but I am not sure that she gained as much as she would have if she had been in school. For us, the last school year was really a year of treading water."

When school started in the fall of 2021, Lisa Juliar's son returned to his high school for an additional year. She still sees daily examples of the ground he lost during school closures. "It used to be that he would do presentations in front of the class. Now he won't even answer a question in front of the class," she said. "He is still not even back to where he was when the pandemic started in many ways." Because most of his friends have moved on to college, he was also faced with the challenge of making new friends. He began spending part of each day at a nearby community college, and that seems to be a good fit, both academically and socially. Next year, he will attend community college full time. But Juliar worries about his friends who are still in fully segregated special education classrooms. She knows that is where her son could have been without her active intervention. But today, she says, "he is blazing his own trail."

Because of the hybrid learning schedule and a relatively quick return to in-person learning, Sarah Johnson says her older daughter seems to have come through the pandemic successfully. "We feel like she'll be just fine," Sarah says.

In contrast, her younger daughter, whose preschool was closed for almost the entire pandemic, is still struggling with a sense of loss. "Two kids in her preschool class left town and she never had a chance to say goodbye." Even after school reopened, she was fearful when winter break approached. "School is closing again," she said. "Will I ever get to go back?"

Margaret and Tom Millar did make the difficult decision to send their son to a private school. They looked for a smaller program that could better meet the needs of diverse learners. Because their son's first-grade learning had been inconsistent, and because he was one of the youngest students in his class, they also decided to have him repeat first grade. "I was just worried about letting him move forward knowing the learning gaps he had." He's happy and "can't wait" to get to school every day, she reports. Ironically, the new school is very close to their old neighborhood, the one they left in search of the right school for their kids.

Once in-person schooling started, Suzann Gallagher saw an instant change in her son. "As soon as he started to go back in person, he was a happier kid. He enjoyed being in a classroom with his teacher. He enjoyed being around other kids. The social aspect alone was worth it."

When the results of the first standardized tests came in, they showed a marked learning loss over the last testing before the COVID school closures. A school administrator told Suzann not to pay attention to the results of a single test, but she frankly was having none of it. "At that point, it was the only data we had. It confirmed what I was seeing myself. He had lost ground."

With the extra support in school and a continuation of the private tutoring, Suzann's son is close to where he was at the start of the pandemic. "It was definitely a lost year. Still, this has been a good year for him. He is consistently a B student. But had we not had that lost year, he would have made more progress."

As her son prepares for middle school, Suzann is hopeful about how well he will do in a new learning environment. "But I can't help wondering—what would he have done if he had had one more year before he started middle school?"

The Wilson family is adjusting to life in Wisconsin. Because of the one-on-one tutoring, her daughter regained her confidence in reading and is doing well in school. They hope to enroll all three children in the outdoor-focused charter school in the upcoming school year. They love the fact that even in the Wisconsin winters, children really do spend much of their day outside. "We've learned the wisdom of the Wisconsin saying that there's no such thing as bad weather, only bad clothing," Wilson says.

Myralyn McCabe and her husband were happy when their son could return to in-person learning. They were grateful for their son's "young, tech-savvy teacher," who helped him stay engaged during the long months of at-home learning. As Myralyn returned to her own classroom, she found a big box of objects her students had created in clay at the beginning of the pandemic. Those students were now in middle school, so the box of unclaimed student art work sits in her classroom as a reminder of the school year she never finished with her students.

When Aimee and Seth Drewry moved their children to a private school, they originally thought it would be for only a year. "We moved here for Fairfax County Public Schools. That's why we are here," Drewry said. "But at the start of the next school year, the school system was again giving off mixed signals about whether they would be open in person or not."

As a result, the family made a decision to stay at the private school. "The school only goes through eighth grade, so I guess we'll have to make another decision then," she said. "But for now, we are happy with the decision."

Kara Stup's son completed two years of virtual learning successfully. As the family was considering his next educational move, which would be to a four-year high school, they asked about the possibility of creating a hybrid schedule. "He does better with virtual learning in some classes," Kara said. "But the ability to socialize and make friends with other students is also important." At the time this book was being finished, the family was "still in negotiation."

Chad and Gabriella Aldeman's two children returned to the Fairfax County Public Schools in the fall of 2021. "They were really happy to be back in school with friends," Chad said. And even though they were not used to wearing masks for seven hours a day, they adjusted pretty quickly.

"Academically," he says, "I think they're fine. We apparently didn't put enough emphasis on geometry for our fourth-grade daughter, so there's a little catch-up happening there. On the other hand, she is definitely ahead of her classmates in some other subjects. Overall, both our kids are in a good place." Professionally, though, Aldeman says he has undergone something of an evolution in how he thinks and writes about public schools. "I'm much more interested," he says, "in finding ways to make schooling more flexible."

Spencer and Krista Potter now have two children in public school. Their eight-year-old, a sociable child, was thrilled to be back in a classroom with other kids and looks forward to getting together for play dates and sleepovers. He is still working on his writing skills (young learners almost all struggled with this small-motor skill).

His younger sister, more of an introvert, is having a bigger adjustment to in-person learning. "She was two when the pandemic first arrived, so she will not remember life before COVID," her father says. "She still prefers to wear a mask even though we tell her it's safe for her to go maskless in most circumstances, now that she's fully vaccinated and COVID has subsided. So much of our psychosocial development and intelligence is premised on the cues we get from seeing other people's faces, and I sometimes worry that her progress in this area might have been delayed since she's been masked up and isolated from peers for so long," Spencer said.

The family's third child was born in December of 2021. Both parents took parental leave, and Krista extended her maternity leave so she could enjoy more time with her children. The family was able to start socializing more openly and "we feel like we're getting our lives back."

Carol and Tom Uecker's grandson was relieved to get back to in-person schooling, although it did take a while to learn how to navigate the hallways in a new school. Orchestra remained one of the highlights of his school day. So in the spring of 2022, he was thrilled to hear from his middle school orchestra teacher, who wondered if he would be interested in starting some private lessons during the summer. He was excited, but he also knew, "I've got to up my game."

Nicole and Eric Christensen's two daughters stayed at the Roots Co-op for two years. But as parents of older students, they decided to return to a more traditional classroom, as there were not enough children to maintain the pod. They made a decision to return to public schools, although given how successful their children had been with Montessori school, they enrolled them in a Montessori charter school in Boulder.

On reflection, the experience was one Christensen says was invaluable. "For my kids, it provided them with consistency and a continuation of some semblance of normal in a time when kids were online and parents were stressed." What she really wants for her kids, she says, is a place where they can "work at their own pace and sometimes choose their own learning activities. There are a lot of different ways to do school, and they can all be really successful."

The three Geller-Cheney kids were all back in the Fairfax County Public Schools for the 2021–2022 school year. They were all happy to be back with their friends. One benefit for the oldest child, Rebecca says, is that the executive skills he developed during the pandemic have stayed with him as he started middle school. "It taught him how to get organized. He saw there was a challenge and he rose to it."

Their middle child, now in fourth grade, also had some positive carryover from his time learning at home. His report card also showed real progress in learning how to manage his time. After two years of doing nearly all her writing on a computer, their second grader needs work on handwriting and other small motor skills. But overall, all three kids are moving forward.

And Rebecca? In the spring of 2022, she was getting a haircut with her regular hairdresser, who said, "You know, you have a lot less gray hair than you did six months ago." Her response: "That's because my kids are back in in-person school."

FINAL THOUGHTS

Shortly before this book is published, schools in this country will start what is effectively Year 4 of the pandemic. The school closures did not lead just to a loss of academic learning. Students missed out on friendships and on exercise and on access to trusted adults who could help them solve problems. Kids with disabilities missed out on the therapy that would help them achieve. And at home, children and parents missed out on time to pay attention to each other while not focusing on work or homework or childcare.

But make no mistake: the learning losses were profound. The more school students missed, the greater their learning loss. And roughly one-fifth of all students were in districts that remained virtual for most of the 2020–21 school year. For the students in the poorest schools, that has resulted in a loss of the equivalent of 22 weeks of instruction.

Now millions of families are leaving public schools. Like the families interviewed for this book, the families in districts that stayed closed the longest are not returning.

Billions of dollars in federal funds are available to schools and districts to address learning loss. But new research in the summer of 2022 found that gaps among groups of students are larger than they were before the pandemic . . . and that the federal money designed to address these losses may run out before the gaps are closed.

Closing those learning gaps is the unfinished learning for all of us.

Unfinished Learning Discussion Guide

Parents, Schools, and the COVID-19 School Closures

1. This book opens with a description of what many different families were doing on the day schools closed because of the coronavirus. Did school closures affect you or your family and friends? Talk about those personal experiences.
2. What do you think of the book's title? The author suggests that talking about "learning loss" is more honest and more accurate than "unfinished learning." What is your opinion?
3. With 20–20 hindsight, is there one thing families could or should have done to prepare for a lengthy period of virtual learning?
4. With that same 20–20 hindsight, is there one thing schools could or should have done to prepare for a lengthy period of virtual learning?
5. One of the themes of the book is that while COVID school closures were challenging for all families, they were especially hard on the students who needed in-person learning the most. What can schools do to help these students in the post-COVID era? How might schools better meet the needs of these students if there are future school closures?
6. How did extended school closures affect families? Do you know families who made big changes in their lives as school closures were extended? Was your family affected? How?
7. Some families set up learning pods as a way of keeping their children in contact with other students while schools were closed. What do you think about learning pods? Are they a helpful way to engage students or do they create greater inequalities?
8. There is growing evidence that some students—particularly low-income students, students with disabilities, and students whose families do not

speak English—suffered much more learning loss than others. How should schools be addressing these disparate needs?

9. During the extended school closures, some families took their children out of public school altogether. Now some of those families are remaining in whatever new situation they chose—private school, home schooling, moving to another school district. Do you know families who left the public schools during COVID? What are they doing now?

10. Parents became much more politically engaged during the pandemic. Did you see this activism in your community? What impact has it had on student learning? Do you see education issues in your community becoming more nationalized? Or are they still focused largely on local issues?

11. Not all the results of COVID school closures were negative. What are some positive changes that could and should be continued even when schools are back to in-person learning?

12. The likelihood is that there will be other school closures in the future. Natural disasters, future pandemics, or other severe local conditions may require schools to close for a period of more than a day or two. What is the advice you would give to school leaders as they plan for these potential future school closures?

Notes

INTRODUCTION

1. B. Dreyer, *Dreyer's English: An Utterly Correct Guide to Clarity and Style* (New York: Random House, 2019), 93.

2. Imperial College of London (2022, July 11). COVID-19 Orphanhood. Retrieved from https://imperialcollegelondon.github.io/orphanhood_calculator/#/country/ United%20States%20of%20America

3. Eliza Griswold (July 13, 2022). The kids who lost parents to COVID. *The New Yorker*. Retrieved from https://www.newyorker.com/news/dispatch/ the-kids-who-lost-parents-to-covid

4. American Academy of Pediatrics, "AAP-AACAP-CHA Declaration of a National Emergency in Child and Adolescent Mental Health," 2021, retrieved from https://www.aap.org/en/advocacy/child-and-adolescent-healthy-mental-development /aap-aacap-cha-declaration-of-a-national-emergency-in-child-and-adolescent-mental -health/.

5. Education Week Research Center, quoted in C. Gewertz, "Teachers Are Losing Hope That This Can Be a Catch-Up Year," *Education Week*, February 8, 2022, retrieved from https://www.edweek.org/leadership/teachers-are-losing-hope-that-this -can-be-a-catch-up-year/2022/02.

6. B. Herold, "How Schools Survived Two Years of COVID-19," *Education Week*, March 15, 2022, retrieved from https://www.edweek.org/teaching-learning/how -schools-survived-two-years-of-covid-19/2022/03.

CHAPTER 1

1. A. Protheroe, "Coronavirus: How Some Schools Are Responding," *Education Week*, January 29, 2020, retrieved from https://www.edweek.org/leadership/ coronavirus-how-some-schools-are-responding/2020/01.

2. N. Messonnier, "CDC Media Telebriefing: Update on COVID-19," Centers for Disease Control, February 25, 2020, retrieved from https://www.cdc.gov/media/releases/2020/a0225-cdc-telebriefing-covid-19.html.

3. A. Schuchat, "Testimony before Senate Health, Education, Labor & Pensions Committee," March 3, 2020, retrieved from https://www.rev.com/blog/transcripts/cdc-officials-testimony-transcript-to-senate-on-coronavirus.

4. M. Lieberman, "Coronavirus Prompting E-learning Strategies," *Education Week*, March 3, 2020, retrieved from https://www.edweek.org/technology/coronavirus-prompting-e-learning-strategies/2020/03.

5. "Map: Coronavirus and School Closures," *Education Week*, April 17, 2020, retrieved from https://www.edweek.org/ew/section/multimedia/map-coronavirus-and-school-closures.html.

6. L. Fishbane and A. Tomer, "As Classes Move Online during COVID-19, What Are Disconnected Students to Do?," Brookings Institution, March 3, 2020, retrieved from https://www.brookings.edu/blog/the-avenue/2020/03/20/as-classes-move-online-during-covid-19-what-are-disconnected-students-to-do/.

7. L. S. Hamilton, J. H. Kaufman, and M. K. Diliberti, *Teaching and Learning through a Pandemic* (Santa Monica, CA: Rand Corporation, 2020), retrieved from file:///C:/Users/kjamu/Downloads/RAND_RRA168-2.pdf.

8. Clea Simon, "How COVID Taught America about Inequity in Education," *Harvard Gazette*, July 2021, retrieved from https://news.harvard.edu/gazette/story/2021/07/how-covid-taught-america-about-inequity-in-education/.

9. Edbuild, *23 Billion* (2019), retrieved from https://edbuild.org/content/23-billion/full-report.pdf. Note: The organization closed in 2020.

10. Quoted in K. Belsha, M. Asmar, and L. Higgins, "'I still just worry': 3 Teachers on Covid's Long Shadow over American Schools," *New York Times*, March 20, 2022, retrieved from https://www.nytimes.com/2022/03/19/sunday-review/pandemic-school-education.html.

11. P. Handwerk, N. Tognatta, R. J. Coley, et al., *Access to Success: Patterns of Advanced Placement Participation in U.S. High Schools* (Educational Testing Service, 2008), retrieved from www.ets.org/Media/Research/pdf/PIC-ACCESS.pdf.

12. Office for Civil Rights *Education in a Pandemic: The Disparate Impacts of COVID-19 on America's Students* (US Department of Education, 2021), retrieved from https://www2.ed.gov/about/offices/list/ocr/docs/20210608-impacts-of-covid19.pdf.

13. E. Hanushek, P. E. Peterson, L. M. Talpey, and L. Woessmann, "Long-Run Trends in the U.S. SES-Achievement Gap," NBER Working Paper No. 26764, National Bureau of Economic Research, retrieved from http://hanushek.stanford.edu/publications/long-run-trends-us-ses-achievement-gap.

14. Murray, P. (2020, March 3). Senate Health, Education, Labor, and Pensions Committee. https://www.rev.com/blog/transcripts/cdc-officials-testimony-transcript-to-senate-on-coronavirus Senate Health, Education, Labor, and Pensions Committee.

15. J. A. Hoffman and E. A. Miller, "Addressing the Consequences of School Closure Due to COVID-19 on Children's Physical and Mental Well-Being," *World Medical & Health Policy*, August 20, 2020, retrieved from https://www.ncbi.nlm.nih.gov/pmc/articles/PMC7461306/#wmh3365-bib-0017.

16. M. Birnbaum, L. Morris, and Q. Aries, "Europe Stays Committed to In-Person Classes as School Outbreaks Remain Rare," *Washington Post*, September 27, 2020, retrieved from https://www.washingtonpost.com/world/europe/coronavirus-outbreaks -schools-europe/2020/09/27/0dd19bf6-ff48-11ea-b0e4-350e4e60cc91_story.html.

17. B. L. Guthrie, D. Tordoff, J. Meisner, et al., "Summary of School Re-opening Models and Implementation Approaches during the COVID 19 Pandemic," Washington State Department of Health, retrieved from https://www.doh.wa.gov/Portals/1/ Documents/1600/coronavirus/20200706-SchoolsSummary.pdf.

18. Birnbaum, et al., "Europe Stays Committed to In-Person Classes."

19. H. B. Stage, J. Shingleton, S. Ghosh, et al., "Shut and Re-open: The Role of Schools in the Spread of COVID-19 in Europe," *Philosophical Transactions of the Royal Society B*, May 31, 2021, retrieved from https://doi.org/10.1101/2020.06.24 .20139634.

20. Donald Trump, Letter to Senate Minority Leader Charles E. Schumer on the federal coronavirus response, April 2, 2020, American Presidency Project, retrieved from https://www.presidency.ucsb.edu/documents/letter-senate-minority-leader -charles-e-schumer-the-federal-coronavirus-response.

21. J. B. Nuzzo and J. M. Sharfstein, "We Have to Focus on Opening Schools, Not Bars," *New York Times*, July 1, 2020, retrieved from https://www.nytimes.com/2020 /07/01/opinion/coronavirus-schools.html.

22. B. Bernhard, "Class Pets Become Long-Term House Guests while Schools Closed," *St. Louis Post-Dispatch*, July 8, 2020, retrieved from https://www .indianagazette.com/leisure/class-pets-become-long-term-house-guests-while -schools-closed/article_9113d762-c123-11ea-92d3-0310d31c484b.html.

CHAPTER 2

1. A. Wong, "Why Millions of Teens Can't Finish Their Homework," *Atlantic*, October 30, 2018, retrieved from https://www.theatlantic.com/education/archive /2018/10/lacking-internet-millions-teens-cant-do-homework/574402/.

2. A. Kline, "During Covid, Schools Have Made a Mad Dash to 1-to-1 Computing: What Happens Next?," *Education Week*, April 20, 2021, retrieved from https://www .edweek.org/technology/during-covid-19-schools-have-made-a-mad-dash-to-1-to-1 -computing-what-happens-next/2021/04.

3. Kline.

4. K. N. Hampton, L. Fernandez, C. T. Robertson, and J. M. Bauer, *Broadband and Student Performance Gaps* (Lansing: James H. and Mary B. Quello Center, Michigan State University, 2020), retrieved from https://quello.msu.edu/broadbandgap/.

5. M. Anderson and M. Perrin, "Nearly One in Five Teens Can't Finish Their Homework Because of the Digital Divide," Pew Research Center, October 26, 2018, retrieved from https://www.pewresearch.org/fact-tank/2018/10/26/nearly-one-in-five -teens-cant-always-finish-their-homework-because-of-the-digital-divide/.

6. Statement of Commissioner Jessica Rosenworcel: "Lifeline and Link Up Reform and Modernization, WC Docket No. 11–42, Telecommunications Carriers Eligible

for Universal Service Support, WC Docket No. 09–197, Connect America Fund, WC Docket No. 10–90," June 28, 2021, retrieved from https://docs.fcc.gov/public/attachments/FCC-16-38A4.pdf.

7. National Center for Education Statistics, *Children's Internet Access at Home* (Washington, DC: U.S. Department of Education, Institute of Education Sciences, 2021), retrieved from https://nces.ed.gov/programs/coe/indicator/cch.

8. Alliance for Excellent Education, "Students of Color Caught in the Homework Gap," Future Ready, 2020, retrieved from https://futureready.org/wp-content/uploads/2020/07/HomeworkGap_FINAL7.20.2020.pdf.

9. The Education Trust (2020). New Statewide Poll of California Parents Finds Satisfaction with Distance Learning Has Declined Significantly. California Parent Poll: 2020. Retrieved from https://west.edtrust.org/california-parent-poll-october-2020/.

10. General Accounting Office, *Distance Learning: Challenges Providing Distance Learning Services to K12 English Learners and Students with Disabilities during COVID-19* General Accounting Offices Reports to Congressional Committees (Washngton, DC: GAO, November 2020), retrieved from https://www.gao.gov/assets/gao-21-43.pdf.

11. US Department of Education Office for Civil Rights, *Education in a Pandemic: The Disparate Impacts of COVID-19 on America's Students* (Washington, DC: US Department of Education, 2021), retrieved from https://www2.ed.gov/about/offices/list/ocr/docs/20210608-impacts-of-covid19.pdf.

12. R. Branstetter, "How Teachers Can Help Students with Special Needs Navigate Distance Learning," *Greater Good Magazine*, October 19, 2020, retrieved from https://greatergood.berkeley.edu/article/item/how_teachers_can_help_students_with_special_needs_navigate_distance_learning.

13. L. Morando-Rhim and S. Ekin, *How Has the Pandemic Affected Students with Disabilities? A Review of the Evidence to Date* (Bothell, WA: Center on Reinventing Public Education, 2021), retrieved from https://www.centerforlearnerequity.org/wp-content/uploads/How-Has-the-Pandemic-Affected-Students-with-Disabilities.pdf.

14. US Department of Education Office for Civil Rights, *Education in a Pandemic.*

15. Advocacy Institute, "New Data: Number of IDEA Eligible Students Ages 3–21 shows Little Change from 2019," *Our Kids Count* (blog), March 8, 2022, retrieved from https://www.advocacyinstitute.org/blog/?p=1043.

16. ParentsTogether Action, "Survey Reveals Remote Learning Is Failing Our Most Vulnerable Students," Parents Together Action, May 27, 2020, retrieved from https://parentstogetheraction.org/2020/05/27/parentstogether-survey-reveals-remote-learning-is-failing-our-most-vulnerablestudents-2/.

17. Morando-Rhim and Ekin, *How Has the Pandemic Affected Students with Disabilities?*

18. T. DiNapoli, *Disruption to Special Education Services: Closing the Gap on Learning Loss from COVID-19* (Albany: New York State Office of the Comptroller, 2021), retrieved from https://www.osc.state.ny.us/files/reports/pdf/special-education-report.pdf.

19. S. Fernandez, "WiFi Buses Were a Quick Solution for Student Internet Access, but as Schools Reopen They Need Their Buses Back," *Texas Tribune*, October 8, 2020, retrieved from https://www.texastribune.org/2020/10/08/schools-internet-buses/.

20. H. Natanson, "Failed Tech, Missed Warnings: How Fairfax Schools' Online Learning Debut Went Sideways," *Washington Post*, April 18, 2020, retrieved from https://www.washingtonpost.com/local/education/fairfax-schools-online-learning -blackboard/2020/04/18/3db6b19c-80b5-11ea-9040-68981f488eed_story.html.

21. A. Goldstein, A. Popescu, and N. Hannah-Jones, "As School Moves Online, Many Students Stay Logged Out," *New York Times*, April 6, 2020, retrieved from https://www.nytimes.com/2020/04/06/us/coronavirus-schools-attendance-absent .html.

22. Healy, M. (April 2022). Missing students. *American School Board Journal.* Retrieved from https://www.nsba.org/ASBJ/2022/april/missing-student.s

23. Gross, B. and Opalka, A. (June 2020). Too many school districts leave learning to chance. Center on Reinventing Public Education. Retrieved from https://crpe.org/ too-many-schools-leave-learning-to-chance-during-the-pandemic/

24. H. T. N. Korman, B. O'Keefe, and M. Repka, "Missing in the Margins 2020: Estimating the scale of the COVID-19 Attendance Crisis," Bellwether Education Partners, 2020 retrieved from https://bellwethereducation.org/publication/missing -margins-estimating-scale-covid-19-attendance-crisis.

25. M. Besecker and A. Thomas, *Student Engagement Online during School Facilities Closures* (Los Angeles: Los Angeles Unified School District, Independent Analysis Unit, July 2020), retrieved from http://laschoolboard.org/sites/default/files /IAU%20Report%202020%200707%20-%20Student%20Engagement%20Online %20During%20Closures.pdf.

26. Hamilton et al., *Teaching and Learning through a Pandemic*.

27. K. McElrath, "Nearly 93% of Households with School-Age Children Report Some Form of Distance Learning during COVID-19," US Census Bureau, retrieved from https://www.census.gov/library/stories/2020/08/schooling-during-the-covid-19 -pandemic.html.

28. Healy, M. (April 2022). Missing students. *American School Board Journal.* Retrieved from https://www.nsba.org/ASBJ/2022/april/missing-students

29. M. Lieberman, "Equity Gaps: Remote Learning Faces Big Challenges," August 24, 2020, *Education Week*, retrieved from https://www.edweek.org/leadership/laptop -delays-zoom-glitches-equity-gaps-remote-learning-faces-big-challenges/2020/08.

30. University of Virginia School of Education and Human Development. (2020). Examining early literacy skills in the wake of COVID-19 Spring 2020 School Disruptions. Retrieved from https://literacy.virginia.edu/sites/g/files/jsddwu1006/files/2022-03/PALS_Fall_2020_Data_Report_5_18_final.pdf.

31. Virginia Department of Education (2021). SOL test pass rates and other results. Retrieved from https://www.doe.virginia.gov/statistics_reports/sol-pass-rates/index. shtml

32. R. Ander, J. Guryan, and J. Ludwig, *Improving Academic Outcomes for Disadvantaged Students: Scaling Up Individualized Tutorials* (Washington, DC: The Hamilton Project, Brookings Institution, 2016), retrieved from https://www .hamiltonproject.org/assets/files/improving_academic_outcomes_for_disadvantaged _students_pb.pdf.

33. US Department of Education Office for Civil Rights, *Education in a Pandemic*.

34. E. Dorn, B. Hancock, J. Sarakatsannis, and E. Viruleg, "COVID-19 and Student Learning in the United States: The Hurt Could Last a Lifetime," McKinsey & Company, June 1, 2020, retrieved from https://www.mckinsey.com/industries/education/our-insights/covid-19-and-student-learning-in-the-united-states-the-hurt-could-last-a-lifetime.

35. Hamilton et al., *Teaching and Learning through a Pandemic*.

36. A. Tadayon, "Letter Grades? Pass/No Pass? A's for All? Districts Differ on Grading Online Learning," EdSource, April 21, 2020, retrieved from https://edsource.org/2020/letter-grades-pass-fail-as-for-all-districts-differ-on-grading-online-learning/629466.

37. S. Sawchuk, "Grading Students during the Coronavirus Crisis: What's the Right Call?," *Education Week*, April 1, 2020, retrieved from https://www.edweek.org/teaching-learning/grading-students-during-the-coronavirus-crisis-whats-the-right-call/2020/04.

38. T. Sedmak, "Fall 2020 College Enrollment Declines 2.5%," National Student Clearinghouse, December 2020, retrieved from https://www.studentclearinghouse.org/blog/fall-2020-college-enrollment-declines-2-5-nearly-twice-the-rate-of-decline-of-fall-2019/.

39. Id.

40. Levinson, M., and Markovits, D. (2022, June). The biggest disruption in the history of American Education. *Atlantic Magazine,* June 23, 2022. Retrieved from https://www.theatlantic.com/ideas/archive/2022/06/covid-learning-loss-remote-school/661360/.

41. Council of the Great City Schools (2022). Marten lauds educators for innovations in face of pandemic. Council of the Great City Schools. *The Urban Educator.* Retrieved from https://www.cgcs.org/Page/1387

42. D. Rahming, "St. Paul School District Provides Food for Kids in Need," *KARE 11*, March 26, 2020, retrieved from https://www.kare11.com/article/news/health/coronavirus/st-paul-public-schools-provide-weekly-meals-for-students-in-need/89-cd99d063-95ac-45fb-a14c-07bc74957110.

43. State of Kansas, Executive Order 20–07, Temporarily closing schools to slow the spread of COVID-19, retrieved from https://governor.kansas.gov/wp-content/uploads/2020/03/EO-20-07-Executed.pdf.

44. B. Lovelace Jr., "CDC Activities and Initiatives Supporting the COVID-19 Response and the President's Plan for Opening America Up Again," CNBC, May 20, 2020. Retrieved from https://www.cnbc.com/2020/05/20/coronavirus-cdc-quietly-releases-detailed-guidelines-for-reopening-us.html.

CHAPTER 3

1. The Education Trust, "Parents Are Overwhelmingly Concerned Their Children Are Falling Behind during School Closures," retrieved from https://edtrust.org/parents-overwhelmingly-concerned-their-children-are-falling-behind-during-school-closures/.

2. E. Dorn, B. Hancock, J. Sarakatsannis, and E. Viruleg, "COVID-19 and Learning Loss: Disparities Grow and Students Need Help," McKinzie & Company, December 8, 2020, retrieved from https://www.mckinsey.com/industries/public-and -social-sector/our-insights/covid-19-and-learning-loss-disparities-grow-and-students -need-help.

3. G. Psacharopoulos, H. Patrinos, et al., "The COVID-19 Cost of School Closures," Brookings Institution, April 2020, retrieved from https://www.brookings.edu/ blog/education-plus-development/2020/04/29/the-covid-19-cost-of-school-closures/.

4. M. Osterholm and M. Olshaker, "It's Too Late to Avoid Disaster, but There Are Still Things We Can Do," *New York Times*, March 27, 2020, retrieved from https: //www.nytimes.com/2020/03/27/opinion/coronavirus-trump-testing-shortages.html.

5. Centers for Disease Control, "Considerations for school closure," July 2020, retrieved from https://www.cdc.gov/coronavirus/2019-ncov/downloads/ considerations-for-school-closure.pdf.

6. M. Birnbaum, L. Morris, and Q. Aries, Europe Stays Committed to In-Person Classes as School Outbreaks Remain Rare. *Washington Post*, September 27, 2020, retrieved from https://www.washingtonpost.com/world/europe/coronavirus-outbreaks -schools-europe/2020/09/27/0dd19bf6-ff48-11ea-b0e4-350e4e60cc91_story.html.

7. H. B. Stage, J. Shingleton, S. Ghosh, F. Scarabel, L. Pellis, and F. Finnie, "Shut and Re-open: The Role of Schools in the Spread of COVID-19 in Europe," June 26, 2020, retrieved from https://doi.org/10.1101/2020.06.24.20139634.

8. J. B. Nuzzo and J. M. Sharfstein, "We Have to Focus on Opening Schools, Not Bars," *New York Times*, July 1, 2020, retrieved from https://www.nytimes.com/2020 /07/01/opinion/coronavirus-schools.html.

9. J. M. Horowitz, "Republicans, Democrats Differ over Factors Schools Should Consider in Deciding Whether to Reopen," Pew Research Center, August 5, 2020, retrieved https://www.pewresearch.org/fact-tank/2020/08/05/republicans-democrats -differ-over-factors-k-12-schools-should-consider-in-deciding-whether-to-reopen/.

10. Horowitz.

11. American Federation of Teachers, "Safely Reopening Schools," July 2020, retrieved from https://www.aft.org/resolution/safely-reopening-schools.

12. Burbio, "In Continued Rise More Than 60% of U.S. K–12 Public School Students Starting School 'Virtually' This Fall," Burbio press release, September 2020, retrieved from https://www.prweb.com/releases/in_continued_rise_more _than_60_of_u_s_k_12_public_school_students_starting_school_virtually_this_fall/ prweb17366345.htm.

13. Bureau of Labor Statistics, "American Time Use Survey, May to December 2019 and 2020," US Department of Labor, July 22, 2021, retrieved from https://www .bls.gov/news.release/pdf/atus.pdf.

14. U. Ranji, B. Frederiksen, et al., "Women, Work and Family during COVID-19: Findings from the KFF Women's Health Survey," Kaiser Family Foundation, 2021, retrieved from https://www.kff.org/womens-health-policy/issue-brief/women-work -and-family-during-covid-19-findings-from-the-kff-womens-health-survey/.

15. National Education Association, "NEA Resolution C-2, Vaccinations," December 2020, retrieved from https://www.nea.org/resource-library/nea-position-covid-19 -vaccines.

16. Education Week, "Where Teachers Are Eligible for the COVID-19 Vaccine," January 2021, retrieved from https://www.edweek.org/policy-politics/where-teachers -are-eligible-for-the-covid-19-vaccine/2021/01.

17. Ko, A. (2021). Interview with author, December 22, 2020.

18. Belsha, K. (2020, October 1). Teaching online? It's an instructional nightmare, some teachers say. *C Chalkbeat.* Retrieved from https://www.chalkbeat. org/2020/10/1/21497795/teaching-in-person-and-virtual-students-at-once-is-an-inst ructional-nightmare-some-educators-say.

19. Kane, T. (2022, May 22). Kids are far, far behind in school. *Atlantic Monthly.* Retrieved from https://www.theatlantic.com/ideas/archive/2022/05/ schools-learning-loss-remote-covid-education/629938/

20. J. Inslee, Emergency Proclamation of the Governor 21–05. State of Washington, Office of the Governor, March 15, 2021, retrieved from https://www.governor.wa .gov/sites/default/files/proclamations/21-05_Children%27s_Mental_Health_Crisis_ %28tmp%29.pdf.

21. National Center for Education Statistics, "Nation's Public School Enrollment Dropped 3 Percent in 2020–21," June 29, 2021, retrieved from https://nces.ed.gov/ whatsnew/press_releases/06_28_2021.asp.

22. M. Burke and D. Willis, "Los Angeles Unified Enrollment Dips Below 600,000, a First in More Than Three Decades," EdSource, April 21, 2020, retrieved from https://edsource.org/2020/los-angeles-unified-enrollment-dips-below-600000-a -first-in-more-than-three-decades/629378.

23. US Census Bureau, "Census Bureau Data Reveal Decline in School Enrollment," October 19, 2021, retrieved from https://www.census.gov/newsroom/press -releases/2021/decline-school-enrollment.html.

24. D. Goldstein and A. Parlapiano, "The Kindergarten Exodus," *New York Times*, August 7, 2021, retrieved from https://www.nytimes.com/2021/08/07/us/covid -kindergarten-enrollment.html.

25. Goldstein and Parlapiano.

26. A. Kamenetz, C. Turner, and M. Khurana, "Where Are the students? For a Second Straight Year, School Enrollment Is Dropping," NPR, December 15, 2021, retrieved from https://www.npr.org/2021/12/15/1062999168/school-enrollment -drops-for-second-straight-year.

27. M. M. Olohan, "Amid Va. Public Schools Discord, Religious Schools See Enrollment Rise," The Heritage Foundation, *The Daily Signal*, retrieved from https://www.dailysignal.com/2021/10/28/religious-virginia-private-schools-surging -enrollment-public-schools-dwindl/.

28. C. Eggleston and J. Fields, "Census Bureau's Household Pulse Survey Shows Significant Increase in Homeschooling Rates in Fall 2020," US Bureau of the Census, March 22, 2021, retrieved from https://www.census.gov/library/stories/2021/03/ homeschooling-on-the-rise-during-covid-19-pandemic.html.

29. A. Jochim and J. Poon, *Crisis Breeds Innovation: Pandemic Pods and the Future of Education* (Seattle, WA: Center for Reinventing Public Education, 2022), retrieved from https://crpe.org/wp-content/uploads/CRPE-Pandemic-Pods-Report_Pages_FINAL.pdf.

30. Jochim and Poon.

31. T. Sedmak, "Fall 2021 Undergraduate Enrollment Declines 465,300 Students Compared to Fall of 2019," National Student Clearinghouse, January 2022, retrieved from https://www.studentclearinghouse.org/blog/fall-2021-undergraduate-enrollment-declines-465300-students-compared-to-fall-2020/.

32. Georgetown University Center on Education and the Workforce, "Three Educational Pathways to Good Jobs," retrieved from https://cew.georgetown.edu/cew-reports/3pathways/.

33. B. Dusseault and T. Pillow, "First Look at ESSER Priorities: Districts Are Placing Their Bets on What They Know," July 2021, Center for Reinventing Public Education, retrieved from https://crpe.org/first-look-at-esser-priorities-districts-are-placing-their-bets-on-what-they-know/.

34. Pew Charitable Trusts, "How State Grants Support Broadband Deployment," Pew Charitable Trusts Broadband Initiative, December 14, 2021, retrieved from https://www.pewtrusts.org/en/research-and-analysis/issue-briefs/2021/12/how-state-grants-support-broadband-deployment.

CHAPTER 4

1. G. A. Coleman, "Challenges Affecting Low-Income Communities' Ability to Deliver and Sustain Virtual Education during the COVID-19 Crisis," Yale School of Medicine, May 29, 2020, retrieved from https://medicine.yale.edu/news-article/challenges-affecting-low-income-communities-ability-to-deliver-and-sustain-virtual-education-during-the-covid-19-crisis/.

2. Imperial College of London, "COVID-19 Orphanhood," 2022, retrieved from https://imperialcollegelondon.github.io/orphanhood_calculator/#/country/United%20States%20of%20America.

3. N. Issa, "Lightfoot Talking to Lyft, Uber after Bus Drivers Quit over Vaccine Mandate," *Chicago Sun-Times*, August 30, 2021, retrieved from https://chicago.suntimes.com/education/2021/8/30/22648862/cps-school-bus-driver-vaccine-mandate-uber-lyft-lightfoot-public-schools.

4. J. Barton, "Retired FBI Executive Michael Mason Hits the Road in a 'Critically Important' Role—Driving a County School Bus," *Chesterfield Observer*, November 10, 2021, retrieved from https://www.chesterfieldobserver.com/articles/retired-fbi-executive-michael-mason-hits-the-road-in-a-critically-important-role-driving-a-county-school-bus/.

5. A. B. Hanson and L. Whitehurst, "Bus Driver Shortages Are Latest Challenge Hitting U.S. Schools," Associated Press, August 22, 2021, retrieved from https://apnews.com/article/coronavirus-pandemic-schools-bus-drivers-168e1e85a329c74159c9f06a05d1611d.

6. N. Modan, "NCES: Nearly Half of Public Schools Impacted by Staffing Shortages, Resignations," K-12 Dive/Wire, March 3, 2022, retrieved from https://www.k12dive.com/news/nces-nearly-half-of-public-schools-impacted-by-staffing-shortage-resignat/619732/.

7. M. Corona, "Dear Colleague Letter—Labor Shortages," US Department of Education, December 15, 2021, retrieved from https://oese.ed.gov/files/2021/12/21-0414.DCL_Labor-Shortages.pdf.

8. Andrabi, T., Daniels, B., Das, J. (2020). Human capital accumulation and disasters: Evidence from the Pakistan earthquake of 2005. RISE Working Paper Series.. https://doi.org/10.35489/BSG-RISE-WP_2020/039.

9. Aldeman, C. (2020, July 28). What a 2005 earthquake in Pakistan can teach American educators about learning loss after a disaster. *The 74*. Retrieved from https://www.the74million.org/article/aldeman-what-a-2005-earthquake-in-pakistan-can-teach-american-educators-about-learning-loss-after-a-disaster/.

10. *Household Experiences in America during the Delta Variant Outbreak*, NPR, the Robert Wood Johnson Foundation, and the Harvard T.H. Chan School of Public Health, October 2021, retrieved from https://media.npr.org/assets/img/2021/10/08/national-report-101221-final.pdf.

11. Leonhardt, D. (2022, May 5). 'Not good for learning.' *New York Times*. Retrieved from https://www.nytimes.com/2022/05/05/briefing/school-closures-covid-learning-loss.html

12. Leonhardt.

13. P. Hill, "What Post-Katrina New Orleans Can Teach Schools about Addressing COVID Learning Losses," Center for Reinventing Public Education, April 2020, retrieved from https://crpe.org/what-post-katrina-new-orleans-can-teach-schools-about-addressing-covid-learning-losses/.

14. Hill.

15. K. Lewis and M. Kuhfeld, "Learning during COVID-19: An Update on Student Achievement and Growth at the Start of the 2021–22 School Year," Center for School Studies, NWEA, 2021, retrieved from https://www.nwea.org/content/uploads/2021/12/Learning-during-COVID19-An-update-on-student-achievement-and-growth-at-the-start-of-the-2021-2022-school-year-Research-Brief-DEC21-FP.pdf.

16. Curriculum Associates, "Understanding Student Learning: Insights from Fall 2021," research brief, retrieved from https://www.curriculumassociates.com/-/media/mainsite/files/i-ready/iready-understanding-student-learning-paper-fall-results-2021.pdf.

17. S. Sawchuk and S. D. Sparks, "Kids Are Behind in Math Because of COVID-19. Here's What Research Says Could Help," *Education Week*, December 2, 2020, retrieved from https://www.edweek.org/teaching-learning/kids-are-behind-in-math-because-of-covid-19-heres-what-research-says-could-help/2020/12.

18. S. Durrance, "Giving Elementary School Teachers the Tools to Teach Math Well," Southern Regional Education Board, 2019, retrieved from https://www.sreb.org/blog-post/giving-elementary-teachers-tools-teach-math-well.

19. S. Khan, *The One World Schoolhouse: Education Reimagined* (New York: Twelve Hachette Book Group, 2012), 83.

20. Lewis Kuhfeld, "Learning during COVID-19."

21. C. Spector, "New Stanford Study Finds Reading Skills among Young Students Stalled during the Pandemic," Stanford University, March 9, 2021, retrieved from https://news.stanford.edu/2021/03/09/reading-skills-young-students-stalled-pandemic/.

22. University of Virginia School of Education and Human Development, *Examining the Impact of COVID-19 on the Identification of At-Risk Students: Fall 2021*, PALS State Report, 2021, retrieved from https://pals.virginia.edu/public/pdfs/login/PALS_StateReport_Fall_2021.pdf.

23. R. Siegler, G. J. Duncan, P. E. Davis-Kean, et al., "Early Predictors of High School Mathematics Achievement," *Psychological Science* 23, no. 7 (2012): 691–97, retrieved from https://journals.sagepub.com/doi/abs/10.1177/0956797612440101.

24. Annie E. Casey Foundation, *Double Jeopardy: How Third Grade Reading Skills and Poverty Influence High School Graduation* (Baltimore: Annie E. Casey Foundation, 2012), retrieved from https://www.aecf.org/resources/double-jeopardy.

25. E. Dorn, B. Hancock, and J. Sarakatsannis, "COVID-19 and Education: An Emerging K-Shaped Recovery," McKinzie & Company, December 2021, retrieved from https://www.mckinsey.com/industries/education/our-insights/covid-19-and-education-an-emerging-k-shaped-recovery.

26. Lewis and Kufeld, "Learning during COVID-19."

27. R. Chetty, J. N. Friedman, N. Hendren, et al., "The Economic Impacts of COVID-19: Evidence from a New Public Database Built Using Private Sector Data," research summary, Opportunity Insights, 2020, retrieved from https://opportunityinsights.org/wp-content/uploads/2021/12/tracker_summary.pdf.

28. J. Friedman, "Professor John Friedman Explains How an Economic Tracker Discovered COVID's K-Shaped Recession—and What It Means for America's Schools," *The 74*, 2021, retrieved from https://www.the74million.org/article/watch-professor-john-friedman-explains-how-an-economic-tracker-discovered-covids-k-shaped-recession-and-what-it-means-for-americas-schools/.

29. Morning Consult (2020, April). Public Opinion Tracker. EdChoice public opinion tracker. Retrieved from https://edchoice.morningconsultintelligence.com/assets/31705.pdf

30. N. Jones, S. Vaughn, and L. Fuchs, "Academic Supports for Students with Disabilities," Annenberg Institute for School Reform at Brown University, EdResearch for Recovery, June 2020, retrieved from https://annenberg.brown.edu/sites/default/files/EdResearch_for_Recovery_Brief_2.pdf.

31. Understood, "Understood Study Reveals Academic, Emotional, and Financial Realities and Implications of Remote Learning," Understood.org, May 17, 2021, retrieved from https://www.understood.org/articles/en/understood-study-reveals-academic-emotional-and-financial-realities-and-implications-of-remote-learning/.

32. American Academy of Pediatrics, American Academy of Child and Adolescent Psychiatry, Children's Hospital Association, "AAP-AACAP-CHA Declaration of National Emergency in Child and Adolescent Mental Health," American Academy of Pediatrics, 2021, retrieved from https://www.aap.org/en/advocacy/child-and

-adolescent-healthy-mental-development/aap-aacap-cha-declaration-of-a-national
-emergency-in-child-and-adolescent-mental-health/.

33. C. Vestal, "COVID Harmed Kids' Health—and Schools Are Feeling It." Pew Trusts *Stateline*, November 8, 2021, retrieved from https://www.pewtrusts.org/en /research-and-analysis/blogs/stateline/2021/11/08/covid-harmed-kids-mental-health -and-schools-are-feeling-it.

34. Centers for Disease Control, "Emergency Department Visits for Suspected Suicide Attempts Among Persons Aged 12–25 Years before and after the COVID-19 Pandemic—United States, January 2019–May 2021," CDC Morbidity and Mortality Weekly Report, June 18, 2021, retrieved from https://www.cdc.gov/mmwr/volumes /70/wr/mm7024e1.htm.

35. S. Ho and C. Fassett, "Pandemic Masks Ongoing Child Abuse Crisis as Cases Plummet," Associated Press, March 29, 2021, retrieved from https://apnews.com/ article/coronavirus-children-safety-welfare-checks-decline-62877b94ec68d47bfe285 d4f9aa962e6.

36. E. Barry, "Many Teens Report Emotional and Physical Abuse by Parents during Lockdown," *New York Times*, March 31, 2022, retrieved from https://www.nytimes .com/2022/03/31/health/covid-mental-health-teens.html.

37. Centers for Disease Control, "Adolescent Behaviors and Experiences Survey," Centers for Disease Control, Division of Adolescent and School Health, March 31, 2022, retrieved from https://www.cdc.gov/healthyyouth/data/abes.htm.

38. L. R. Bullinger, A. Boy, M. Feely, S. Messner, K. Raissian, W. Schneider, and S. Self-Brown, "Home, but Left Alone: Time at Home and Child Abuse and Neglect During COVID-19," *Journal of Family Issues*, October 9, 2021, retrieved from https: //doi.org/10.1177/0192513X211048474.

39. E. Coe, K. Enomoto, B. Herbig, et al., "COVID-19 and Burnout Are Straining the Mental Health of Employed Parents," McKinzie and Company, December 2021, retrieved from https://www.mckinsey.com/industries/healthcare-systems -and-services/our-insights/covid-19-and-burnout-are-straining-the-mental-health-of -employed-parents.

40. A. Kamenetz and C. Turner, "Where Are the Students? For a Second Straight Year, Enrollment Is Dropping," National Public Radio, December 15, 2021, retrieved from https://www.npr.org/2021/12/15/1062999168/school-enrollment-drops-for -second-straight-year.

41. P. Esquivel, "Nearly Half of LA Students Chronically Absent This Year, Data Show." *Los Angeles Times*, March 31, 2022, retrieved from https://www.latimes.com/ california/story/2022-03-31/lausd-students-chronic-absent-amid-covid-pandemic.

42. Attendance Works, "Addressing Chronic Absence," retrieved from https://www .attendanceworks.org/chronic-absence/the-problem/.

CHAPTER 5

1. A. Russo, "'Squid Game' School Board Coverage Isn't Helping." *Kappan online*, October 22, 2021, retrieved from https://kappanonline.org/russo-squid-game -coverage-of-school-board-protests/.

2. For this discussion, I am deeply indebted to Nancy R. Hamant's "Religion in the Cincinnati Schools, 1830–1900," *Bulletin of the Historical and Philosophical Society of Ohio*, 10 (1963): 239–51, retrieved from http://library.cincymuseum.org/journals/files/hpsobull/v21/n4/hpsobull-v21-n4-rel-239.pdf.

3. Hamant.

4. N. Piediscalzi, "Studying Religion in the Public Schools," *Church & State*, November 1981, 14.

5. The sentiment was perhaps a bit over the top, but how often does one hear "calumniate" in any sort of civic discourse?

6. C. S. Reinhart, "A Foreign Demand," *Harper's Weekly*, September 27, 1873, retrieved from https://art.famsf.org/charles-stanley-reinhart/foreign-demand-harpers -weekly-september-27-1873-cover-page-19633019121.

7. *Board of Education of the City of Cincinnati v. Minor,* Ohio S. Ct. (1872).

8. R. Halliburton, "Kentucky's Anti-Evolution Controversy," *Register of the Kentucky Historical Society*, 66, no. 2 (1968): 97–107, retrieved from http://www.jstor .org/stable/23377065.

9. G. Branch, "One Hundred Years of Anti-evolution Are More Than Enough," *Religion Dispatches*, March 4, 2022, retrieved from https://religiondispatches.org/one -hundred-years-of-anti-evolution-legislation-are-more-than-enough/.

10. Public Acts of the State of Tennessee, AN act prohibiting the teaching of the Evolution Theory in all the Universities, Normals and all other public schools of Tennessee, which are supported in whole or in part by the public school funds of the State, and to provide penalties for the violations thereof, 1925, retrieved from http:// law2.umkc.edu/faculty/projects/ftrials/scopes/tennstat.htm.

11. J. Lepore, "Why the School Wars Still Rage," *New Yorker*, retrieved from https: //www.newyorker.com/magazine/2022/03/21/why-the-school-wars-still-rage.

12. N. Adams, "Timeline: Remembering the Scopes Monkey Trial," National Public Radio, July 2005, retrieved from https://www.npr.org/2005/07/05/4723956/ timeline-remembering-the-scopes-monkey-trial.

13. P. Edwards, "The Scopes Monkey Trial Was One of the Greatest Publicity Stunts Ever," *Vox*, retrieved from https://www.vox.com/2015/7/21/9009713/scopes -trial-spectacle.

14. C. W. Puckett, "The Evolution Arena at Dayton," *New York Times*, 89, 110.

15. R. O'Harrow, "Creationism Issue Evolves in Fairfax School Election," October 21, 1995, *Washington Post*, retrieved from https://www.washingtonpost.com/archive /politics/1995/10/21/creationism-issue-evolves-in-fairfax-school-election/52b2bb92 -ee24-4347-aa07-6e83f48fd4b8/.

16. J. Duvall, "School Board Tackles Creationism Debate," CNN, November 5, 1995, retrieved from http://www.cnn.com/US/9511/creationism/index.html.

17. American Family Association, cited in M. M. Deckman, *School Board Battles: The Christian Right in Local Politic* (Washington, DC: Georgetown University Press, 2004), 116.

18. J. Holcomb, T. Hartson, Y. Kim, et al., *Keeping Up with the Ed Beat: How News Habits, Racial Identity, and a Public Health Crisis Have Shaped Parents' Experience with Education News*, William & Flora Hewlett Foundation, February, 2022, retrieved

from https://calvin.edu/centers-institutes/center-for-social-research/projects-services
/education-news/files/Education%20News%20Survey%20Report%2020220216.pdf.

19. D. S. Massey and J. Tannen, "Suburbanization and Segregation in the United
States: 1970–2010," *Ethnic and Racial Studies 41, no.* 9 (2018): 1594–611, retrieved
from https://doi.org/10.1080/01419870.2017.1312010.

20. Massey D. S., Tannen J. Suburbanization and Segregation in the United States:
1970–2010. *Ethn Racial Stud.* 2018;41(9):1594–1611. Retrieved from https://www.
ncbi.nlm.nih.gov/pmc/articles/PMC6145815/.

21. Loudoun County Public Schools (2021). 2021–2022 Fact Sheet. Retrieved from
https://www.lcps.org/Page/235155.

22. D. Sosnik, "America's Suburbs: Ground Zero in 21st Century Politics," Politico
Playbook, 2022, retrieved from https://www.politico.com/playbook.

23. H. Natanson, "A Lost History Recovered: Faded Records Tell the Story of
School Segregation in Virginia," *Washington Post*, February 2, 2020, retrieved from
https://www.washingtonpost.com/local/education/a-lost-history-recovered-faded
-records-tell-the-story-of-school-segregation-in-virginia/2020/02/22/.

24. M. R. Herring, "Letter to Loudoun County Public Schools Regarding OCR
Case No.: 19–2652, NAACP Loudoun Branch v. Loudoun County Public Schools,"
Office of the Virginia Attorney General, February 8, 2021, retrieved from https://s3
.documentcloud.org/documents/20784650/lcps-resolution_agreement.pdf.

25. Loudoun County Public Schools, *A Way Forward Together: Equity Workshop.*
BoardDocs, 2021, retrieved from https://go.boarddocs.com/vsba/loudoun/Board
.nsf/files/C3KTHK760E4E/$file/SB%20BoardDocs%20Equity%20Workshop%20-
%20Promise%2C%20Progress%20and%20the%20Path%20Forward.pdf.

26. L. G. Streeter, "'A Dog Whistle and a Lie': Black Parents on the Critical Race
Theory Debate." *Washington Post*, December 7, 2021, retrieved from https://www
.washingtonpost.com/parenting/2021/12/07/black-parents-crt-race/.

27. Heritage Foundation, "Citizens Guide to Fight for America: School Boards
Hold the Keys to Local Education," 2021, retrieved from https://www.heritage.org
/citizens-guide-fight-america/2021-action-items/school-boards-hold-the-keys-local
-education.

28. The Manhattan Institute, "Woke Schooling: A Toolkit for Concerned Parents," retrieved from https://www.manhattan-institute.org/woke-schooling-toolkit-for
-concerned-parents.

29. A. Kamenetz, "A Look at the Groups Aiding Protests against Masks, Vaccines,
and Critical Race Theory," National Public Radio, retrieved from https://www.npr.org
/2021/10/26/1049078199/a-look-at-the-groups-supporting-school-board-protesters
-nationwide.

30. Parents Defending Education, "Resolution of the Paso Robles Joint Unified
School District Prohibiting the Teaching of Critical Race Theory," retrieved from
https://defendinged.org/resources/resolution-of-the-paso-robles-joint-unified-school
-district-prohibiting-the-teaching-of-critical-race-theory/.

31. Turning Point USA, "School Board Watchlist," retrieved from https://www
.schoolboardwatchlist.org/.

32. Federal Elections Commission, "Report of Receipts and Disbursements, the 1776 Project Political Action Committee," retrieved from https://docquery.fec.gov/cgi-bin/forms/C00764860/1541435/.

33. Moms for Liberty, "How to Submit an Open Records Request," retrieved from https://www.momsforliberty.org/resources/.

34. B. Wallace-Wells, "How a Conservative Activist Invented the Conflict over Critical Race Theory," *New Yorker*, June 18, 2021, retrieved from https://www.newyorker.com/news/annals-of-inquiry/how-a-conservative-activist-invented-the-conflict-over-critical-race-theory.

35. Kamenetz, "A Look at the Groups."

36. "Tucker: America Is at an Inflection Point," Transcript of November 3, 2021, Fox News program, retrieved from https://www.foxnews.com/transcript/tucker-america-is-at-an-inflection-point.

37. Photograph by K. Frey, in *Washington Post*, November 3, 2021, retrieved from https://www.washingtonpost.com/local/education/parent-control-schools-republican-virginia/2021/11/03/313e8a68-3cc3-11ec-a493-51b0252dea0c_story.html.

38. Wallace-Wells, "How a Conservative Activist Invented the Conflict over Critical Race Theory."

39. T. Okun, "Dismantling White Supremacy Culture," Dismantlingracism.org., 2020, retrieved from https://www.whitesupremacyculture.info/uploads/4/3/5/7/43579015/okun_-_white_sup_culture_2020.pdf.

40. T. L. Green and N. Hagiwara, "The Problem with Implicit Bias Training," *Scientific American*, August 28, 2020, retrieved from https://www.scientificamerican.com/article/the-problem-with-implicit-bias-training/.

41. Parents Defending Education, "Consultants Report: The Equity Collaborative," 2021, retrieved from https://defendinged.org/report/the-equity-collaborative/

42. Parents Against Critical Theory, "What Is CRT and Its Impact on Loudoun County Schools?," The Virginia Project, 2021, retrieved from https://stoplcpscrt.com/2021/03/03/3-3-21-the-va-project-and-p-a-c-t-present-what-is-crt-and-its-impact-on-loudoun-county-schools/.

43. E. Richards, and A. Wong, "Parents Want Kids to Learn about Ongoing Effects of Slavery—but Not Critical Race Theory. They're the Same Thing," *USA Today*/Ipsos poll, *USA Today*, retrieved from https://www.usatoday.com/story/news/education/2021/09/10/crt-schools-education-racism-slavery-poll/5772418001/.

44. H. Natanson, "How and Why Loudoun County Became the Face of the Nation's Culture Wars," July 5, 2021, *Washington Post*, retrieved from https://www.washingtonpost.com/local/education/loudoun-critical-race-theory-transgender-rights/2021/07/05/3dab01b8-d4eb-11eb-ae54-515e2f63d37d_story.html.

45. Code of Virginia. § 22.1–23.3, retrieved from https://law.lis.virginia.gov/vacode/22.1-23.3/.

46. Loudoun County School Board, Draft—Policy 8040, Rights of Transgender and Gender-Expansive Students, Loudoun County Public Schools, 2021, retrieved from https://loudounnow.com/wp-content/uploads/2021/05/Draft-POLICY_-8040-Rights-of-Transgender-Students-5-6-21.pdf.

47. Jouvenal, J. (2021, October 25). In case at center of political firestorm, judge finds teen committed sexual assault in Virginia school bathroom. *Washington Post*. Retrieved from https://www.washingtonpost.com/local/public-safety/in-case-at-center-of-political-firestorm-judge-finds-teen-committed-sexual-assault-in-virginia-school-bathroom/2021/10/25/42c037da-35cc-11ec-8be3-e14aaacfa8ac_story.html.

48. J. Singal, "Police Logs Contradict Some of *The Daily Wire*'s Reporting on the Loudoun County Rape Scandal," Blocked and Reported.org., October 2021, retrieved from https://www.blockedandreported.org/p/police-logs-contradict-some-of-the.

49. B. DeVos, "Secretary DeVos Takes Historic Action to Strengthen Title IX Protection for All Students," US Department of Education press release, retrieved from https://content.govdelivery.com/accounts/USED/bulletins/28a2d60.

50. US Senate Committee on Health, Education, Labor, and Pensions, "Senator Murray Slams Secretary DeVos's Title IX Rule, Calls On the Department to Focus on COVID-19 Response," May 2020, retrieved from https://www.help.senate.gov/ranking/newsroom/press/senator-murray-slams-secretary-devos-title-ix-rule-calls-on-the-department-to-focus-on-covid-19-response.

51. T. Cotton, "Sen. Tom Cotton vs. AG Merrick Garland on Loudoun Bathroom Assault: 'Thank God You Are Not on the Supreme Court.'" RealClear Politics, video from CSPAN-#, October 27, 2021, retrieved from https://www.realclearpolitics.com/video/2021/10/27/sen_tom_cotton_at_ag_garland_on_school_boards_issue_thank_god_you_are_not_on_the_supreme_court.html.

52. Virginia Legislative Information System (2022). House Bill 781, retrieved from https://lis.virginia.gov/cgi-bin/legp604.exe?221+ful+HB781&fbclid=IwAR2-GhSIi5O_Bv2v85y_p42cWG4axWdNX0PZvvMz1G1Gj4BqyZwfAOTO5E8.

53. D. Strain, "Angry Politicians Make Angry Voters, Study Finds," University of Colorado, *CU Boulder Today*, retrieved from https://www.colorado.edu/today/2021/07/16/angry-politicians-make-angry-voters-new-study-finds.

54. 457 U.S. 853 (1982).

55. PEN America, "Banned in the USA: Rising School Book Bans Threaten Free Expression And Students' First Amendment Rights," 2022, retrieved from https://pen.org/banned-in-the-usa/#policies.

56. American Library Association, "Guidelines for Reconsideration Committees," retrieved from https://www.ala.org/tools/challengesupport/reconsiderationcommittees.

57. Fairfax County Public Schools, Regulation 3009.11, Challenged library and instructional materials, 2021, retrieved from https://go.boarddocs.com/vsba/fairfax/Board.nsf/files/C2BQFE68F029/$file/R3009.pdf.

58. R. Kopetman, "Effort to Ban Critical Race Theory Could Jeopardize AP Classes in Placentia-Yorba Linda Schools," *Orange County Register*, March 22, 2022, retrieved from https://www.ocregister.com/2022/03/22/a-proposal-to-shape-the-teaching-of-race-raises-questions-fear-of-losing-ap-classes-in-placentia-yorba-linda-schools/.

59. Placentia-Yorba Linda School District, Resolution No. 21–12: Resolution concerning district teaching of critical race theory (CRT) as a framework on matters relating to race, April 5, 2022, retrieved from https://4.files.edl.io/c30b/04/06/22/194827-8344512a-9061-418d-a3f9-14e0b380fdb4.pdf.

60. Red Wine & Blue, "Book Ban Busters," retrieved from https://www.redwine .blue/bbb.

61. E. Delmore, "With Book Bans on the Rise, Moms Who Oppose Them Are Pushing Back," MSNBC, retrieved from https://www.msnbc.com/know-your-value /out-of-office/book-bans-tennessee-texas-florida-moms-against-them-are-pushing -n1290647.

62. Arrington, R. (2022, January). Luray parent charged after "threatening" statement at school board meeting. *Page Valley News.* Retrieved from https://pagevalleynews. com/luray-parent-charged-after-threatening-statement-at-school-board-meeting/

CHAPTER 6

1. Centers for Disease Control, "Nearly 80 Percent of Teachers, School Staff, and Childcare Workers Receive at least One Shot of COVID-19 Vaccine," CDC Online Newsroom, retrieved from https://www.cdc.gov/media/releases/2021/s0406-teachers -staff-vaccine.html.

2. C. Aldeman, "How Much Learning Time Are Students Getting? In 7 Large School Districts, Less Than Normal—and in 3, They're Getting More," *The 74*, October 20, 2020, retrieved from https://www.the74million.org/article/aldeman -how-much-learning-time-are-students-getting-in-7-large-school-districts-less-than -normal-and-in-3-theyre-getting-more/.

3. Asher Leher-Small, "One Fate, Two Fates, Red States, Blue States: New Data Reveal a 432-Hour In-Person Learning Gap Produced by the Politics of Pandemic Schooling," *The 74*, June 9, 2021, retrieved from https://www.the74million .org/article/one-fate-two-fates-red-states-blue-states-new-data-reveals-a-432-hour-in -person-learning-gap-produced-by-the-politics-of-pandemic-schooling/.

4. C. Daniels, "Seattle Students 2nd Grade and Older May Not Return in Person until Fall," KING5-TV February 12, 2021, retrieved from https://www.king5 .com/article/news/health/coronavirus/seattle-schools-cdc-reopening-guidance/281 -05f18bf1-6a30-488c-9a6e-6a695adac356.

5. J. Inslee, Emergency proclamation of the Governor 21–05, retrieved from https://www.governor.wa.gov/sites/default/files/proclamations/21-05_Children%27s _Mental_Health_Crisis_%28tmp%29.pdf.

6. A. Dornfield, "'Now Is the Time.' Gov. Inslee Orders Washington Schools to Reopen by April 19," KUOW, March 12, 2021, retrieved from https://www.kuow.org /stories/now-is-the-time-wash-gov-jay-inslee-orders-schools-to-reopen-by-apr-19th.

7. M. Drouin, B. T. McDaniel, J. Pater, J., and T. Toscos, "How Parents and Their Children Used Social Media and Technology at the Beginning of the COVID-19 Pandemic and Associations with Anxiety," *Cyberpsychology, Behavior and Social Networking* 23, no. 11 (2020): 727–36, retrieved from https://doi.org/10.1089/cyber .2020.0284.

8. Tim Pierce, "Online Parenting Communities Pulled Closer to Extreme Groups Spreading Disinformation during COVID-19 Pandemic," George Washington University, January 23, 2022, retrieved from https://mediarelations.gwu.edu/online

-parenting-communities-pulled-closer-extreme-groups-spreading-misinformation
-during-covid-19.

9. NPR, "Parents' COVID Frustrations Are a Political Issue for Democrats,"
Politics Podcast February 22, 2022, retrieved from https://www.npr.org/transcripts
/1082380654.

10. Hitler perfected the blitzkrieg in Spain. Picasso's painting *Guernica* commemo-
rates the devastation of the German bombing of that city.

11. A. Blake, "New Poll Shows GOP Nullifying Democrats' Edge on Education,"
Washington Post, November 15, 2021, retrieved from https://www.washingtonpost
.com/politics/2021/11/15/new-poll-shows-gop-nullifying-democrats-edge-education/.

12. N. Corasaniti, "National Issues Dominate Ad Wars in Virginia Governor's
Race," *New York Times*, October 12, 2021, retrieved from https://www.nytimes.com
/2021/10/12/us/politics/virginia-governor-campaign-ads.html.

13. McAuliffe for Governor Campaign, "Election Results Analysis," Blue Virginia, November 5, 2021, retrieved from https://bluevirginia.us/2021/11/mcauliffe
-campaign-post-election-memo-dems-saw-historic-turnout-but-youngkin-capitalized
-on-the-democratic-stalemate-and-the-fox-news-conservative-media-echo-chamber
-to-drive-turnout-from-he.

14. Washington Post–Schar School, "Washington Post–Schar School Virginia
Poll," *Washington Post*, October 2021, retrieved from https://www.washingtonpost
.com/context/oct-20-26-2021-washington-post-schar-school-virginia-poll/1ad60e58
-0bc2-404d-80e6-0f8ff5fba246/.

15. Democrats for Education Reform & Murmuration, "Poll Confirms Education Motivating Issue for VA Voters in 2021 Election; Likely to Be Major Factor in
Midterms," November 22, 2021, retrieved from https://dfer.org/press/poll-confirms
-education-motivating-issue-for-va-voters-in-2021-election-likely-to-be-major-factor
-in-midterms/.

16. Democrats for Education Reform & Murmuration.

17. Institute for Social Research, "Anger Motivates People to Vote, U-M Study
Shows," University of Michigan, 2011, retrieved from https://isr.umich.edu/news
-events/insights-newsletter/article/anger-motivates-people-to-vote-u-m-study-shows/.

18. McKend, A., & Merica, D. (2021, October 7). Virginia Republicans seize on
parental rights and schools fight in final weeks of campaign. CNN. Retrieved from
https://www.cnn.com/2021/10/07/politics/glenn-youngkin-parental-rights-education-
strategy/index.html.

19. Corasaniti, "National Issues Dominate Ad Wars."

20. Martin, J., & Burns, A. (2021, November 6). Reeling from surprise losses,
Democrats sound the alarm for 2022. *New York Times*. Retrieved from https://www.
nytimes.com/2021/11/03/us/politics/democrat-losses-2022.html

21. Democrats for Education Reform & Murmuration, "Poll Confirms Education
Motivating Issue."

22. CNN, "Live CNN Exit Polls—Virginia," November 2021, retrieved from https:
//www.cnn.com/election/2021/november/exit-polls/virginia/governor/0.

23. Kennedy, R. F. (1963, March 18). Address at Kentucky's Centennial of the Emancipation Proclamation. U.S. Department of Justice Archives. Retrieved from https://www. Justice.gov/sites/default/files/ag/legacy/2011/01/20/03-18-1963Pro.pdf.

24. C. F. Rufo on Twitter, https://twitter.com/realchrisrufo/status /1455696705576390658.

25. A. Seitz-Wald, "Democrats See Lessons from Virginia Defeat, but Strategists Worry Party Isn't Listening," NBC News, November 15, 2021, retrieved from https://www.nbcnews.com/politics/elections/democrats-see-lessons-virginia-defeat -strategists-worry-party-isn-t-n1283816.

26. D. Montenaro, "A Bad Omen for Democrats and 4 Other Election Night Takeaways," National Public Radio, retrieved from https://www.npr.org/2021/11/03 /1051713890/election-analysis-virginia-new-jersey-democrats.

27. N. Wallace, retrieved from https://www.nbcnews.com/politics/elections/ democrats-see-lessons-virginia-defeat-strategists-worry-party-isn-t-n1283816 https: //twitter.com/townhallcom/status/1455693642866298887.

28. B. Stryker and O. Savir, "Qualitative Research Findings: Virginia Post-election Research," ALG Research, Third Way, November 15, 2021, retrieved from https://thirdway.imgix.net/pdfs/override/ Qualitative-Research-Findings—Virginia-Post-Election-Research.pdf.

29. W. Saletan, "What the Polls Really Tell Us about How Critical Race Theory Affected the Virginia Election," *Slate Magazine*, November 5, 2021, retrieved from https://slate.com/news-and-politics/2021/11/polls-critical-race-theory-virginia -election.html.

30. Stryker Savir, "Qualitative Research Findings."

31. Democrats for Education Reform & Murmuration, "Poll Confirms Education Motivating Issue."

32. S. Isgur and C. Stirewalt, "The Sweep: Takeaway from Glenn Youngkin's Victory in Virginia," *The Dispatch*, November 3, 2021, retrieved from https://sweep .thedispatch.com/p/the-sweep-the-takeaway-from-youngkins?s=r.

33. D. Barefoot on Twitter. The thread is no longer available, but a news story discussing it can be retrieved from the Seitz-Wald story referenced above.

34. Democrats for Education Reform & Murmuration, "Poll Confirms Education Motivating Issue."

35. J. M. Horowitz, "Republicans, Democrats Differ over Factors Schools Should Consider in Deciding Whether to Reopen," Pew Research Center, August 5, 2020, retrieved https://www.pewresearch.org/fact-tank/2020/08/05/republicans-democrats -differ-over-factors-k-12-schools-should-consider-in-deciding-whether-to-reopen/.

36. Z. D. Carter, "The Democratic Unraveling Began with Schools," *Atlantic* November 3, 2021, retrieved from https://www.theatlantic.com/ideas/archive/2021 /11/virginia-election-youngkin-education/620596/.

37. See note 30.

38. A. Kamenetz, "Why Education Was a Top Voter Priority This Election," National Public Radio, November 1, 2021, retrieved from https://www.npr.org/2021 /11/04/1052101647/education-parents-election-virginia-republicans.

39. M. Kruse, "The Parental Revolution Is Bigger Than Critical Race Theory," *Politico*, November 9, 2021, retrieved from https://www.politico.com/news/magazine/2021/11/09/the-parental-revolution-we-all-saw-coming-but-still-missed-520450.

40. *Playbook Deep Dive,* February 11, 2022, "The Gen X Activists Upending Democratic Politics," retrieved from https://podcasts.apple.com/nl/podcast/the-gen-x-activists-upending-democratic-politics/id1111319839?i=1000550782734.

41. O. F. Taylor, "Race, Class, Legacy, and Logistics: The Failed Project to rename San Francisco's Public Schools," *Columbia Political Review*, April 18, 2021, retrieved from http://www.cpreview.org/blog/2021/4/race-class-legacy-and-logistics-the-failed-project-to-rename-san-franciscos-public-schools.

42. *Playbook Deep Dive*, "The Gen X Activists."

43. L. Breed, News Release: Statement from Mayor London Breed on school renaming, retrieved from https://sfmayor.org/article/statement-mayor-london-breed-school-renaming.

44. San Francisco Unified School District, "Timeline for Returning to In-Person Learning," April 2021, retrieved from https://www.sfusd.edu/covid-19-response-updates-and-resources/preparing-fall-2021/archived-timeline-returning-person-learning.

45. San Francisco Unified School District, "SF Board of Education Commits to Returning All Students to Full-Time In-Person Learning for Fall 2021," April 7, 2021, retrieved from https://www.sfusd.edu/about-sfusd/sfusd-news/current-news-sfusd/sf-board-education-commits-returning-all-students-full-time-person-learning-fall-2021.

46. California School Dashboard, "School Performance Overview: Lowell High School," 2020, retrieved from https://www.caschooldashboard.org/reports/38684783833407/2020.

47. M. Burke, "Enrollment at San Francisco Schools Declines by 3500 Students," EdSource, October 12, 2021, retrieved from https://edsource.org/updates/enrollment-at-san-francisco-schools-declines-by-3500-students.

48. M. Barba, "SF School Board Members Break Silence as Recalls Ramp Up," *San Francisco Examiner*, August 20, 2021, retrieved from https://www.sfexaminer.com/news/sf-school-board-members-break-their-silence-as-recall-ramps-up/.

49. S. Hinckley, "Why Are Parents So Mad in One of America's Best School Districts?," *Christian Science Monitor*, May 27, 2021, retrieved from https://www.csmonitor.com/USA/Politics/2021/0527/Why-are-parents-so-mad-in-one-of-America-s-best-school-districts.

50. "School Board Recalls," Ballotopedia, 2022, retrieved from https://ballotpedia.org/School_board_recalls.

51. A. Johnson and R. Linnane, "Mequon-Thiensville Recall Fails to Unseat Any School Board Members after High-Spending race with National Attention," *Milwaukee Journal Sentinel*, November 2, 2021, retrieved from https://www.jsonline.com/story/communities/northshore/news/mequon/2021/11/02/mequon-thiensville-school-board-recall-election-results-november-2-2021/6250162001/.

52. T. Flores, "Electors Slash Kenosha School Board Salaries, Recommend Nearly $1.2 Million Decrease in Property Tax Levy," Madison.com, retrieved from https:

//madison.com/news/local/education/local_schools/electors-slash-kenosha-school
-board-salaries-recommend-nearly-1-2m-decrease-in-proposed-tax-levy/article
_13b18b15-8261-591f-8ed2-43c76f950786.html.

53. W. McKenzie, "Strong Local Newspapers Are a Key to Strengthening Our Democracy," The George W. Bush Institute, 2022, retrieved from https://www
.bushcenter.org/catalyst/restoring-trust-in-institutions/mckenzie-strong-newspapers
-strong-democracy.html.

54. "Governor Ducey: 'In-Person Learning Will Continue in Arizona,'" Office of the Arizona Governor, News Release, January 4, 2022, retrieved from https://azgovernor
.gov/governor/news/2022/01/governor-ducey-person-learning-will-continue-arizona.

55. B. Olneck-Brown, "States Make School Choice Part of COVID-Era Education Response," National Conference of State Legislatures, *State Legislatures News*, April 21, 2021, retrieved from https://www.ncsl.org/research/education/states-make-private
-school-choice-part-of-covid-era-education-response-magazine2021.aspx.

56. M. Bloomberg, "Michael Bloomberg: Why I'm Backing Charter Schools," *Wall Street Journal*, December 1, 2021, retrieved from https://www.wsj.com/
articles/michael-bloomberg-why-im-backing-charter-schools-covid-19-learning-loss
-teachers-union-11638371324.

CHAPTER 7

1. N. Silver, on Twitter, January 11, 2002, https://twitter.com/natesilver538/status
/1480986849506123780?lang=en.

2. Suffolk University/USA Today Polls, National Poll with USA Today Marginals, January 10, 2022, retrieved from https://www.suffolk.edu/-/media/suffolk/documents
/academics/research-at-suffolk/suprc/polls/national/2022/01_10_2022_complete
_marginals.pdf.

3. J. McGahan, "Exclusive: Cecily Myart-Cruz's Hostile Takeover of L.A.'s Public Schools," *Los Angeles Magazine*, retrieved from https://www.lamag.com/
citythinkblog/cecily-myart-cruz-teachers-union/.

4. Washington Post Editorial Board. "Yes, We'll Have No Banana," *Washington Post*, December 3, 1978, retrieved from https://www.washingtonpost.com
/archive/opinions/1978/12/03/yes-well-have-no-banana/ff66f487-7e1a-4579-a199
-5750373405c9/.

5. P. Wall, "'War on Learning Loss': Newark Teachers Union Calls for Citywide Effort to Catch Students Up." Chalkbeat Newark, April 1, 2022, retrieved from https://
newark.chalkbeat.org/2022/4/1/23006974/newark-teachers-union-learning-loss-war.

6. C. Pitts, T. Pillow, B. Dusseault, and R. Lake, "Virtual Learning: Now and Beyond," Center on Reinventing Public Education, January 2022, retrieved from https://www.covidcollaborative.us/assets/uploads/img/final2-Virtual-learning-post
-COVID-report.pdf.

7. National Digital Inclusion Alliance, *Digital Inclusion Coalition Guidebook*, 2022, retrieved from https://www.digitalinclusion.org/blog/2022/02/24/ndia-publishes-new
-digital-inclusion-coalition-guidebook/.

8. K. Bateman and L. McKittrick, Virtual IEPs Should Stay, Center on Reinventing Public Education, April 2021, retrieved from https://crpe.org/virtual-ieps-should-stay/.

9. R. L. Slavin, "Launching ProvenTutoring," *Robert Slavin's Blog*, April 26, 2021, retrieved from https://robertslavinsblog.wordpress.com/tag/tutoring/.

10. J. Kaufman and M. Diliberti, "Teachers Are Not All Right: How the COVID-19 Pandemic Is Taking a Toll on the Nation's Teachers," Center for Reimagining Public Education, The Evidence Project at CRPE, January 2021, retrieved from https://crpe.org/wp-content/uploads/final-EP-teachers-synthesis.pdf.

11. To learn more about using playlists to differentiate student learning, see https://www.cultofpedagogy.com/student-playlists-differentiation/.

12. Next Education Workforce, "SPARK School: Covid addendum," Mary Lou Fulton Teachers College, Arizona State University, 2021, retrieved from https://www.cultofpedagogy.com/student-playlists-differentiation/.

13. National School Boards Association, "The Public's Voice," retrieved from https://www.nsba.org/ASBJ/2020/April/the-publics-voice.

14. C. Rufo, on Twitter, November 2, 2021, retrieved from https://twitter.com/realchrisrufo/status/1455696705576390658.

15. B. Wickler, Twitter, April 8, 2022, retrieved from https://twitter.com/benwikler/status/1512515301501456386.

16. Loudoun County School Board, LEAF Charter—Final, Loudoun County Public Schools, April 1, 2022, retrieved from https://go.boarddocs.com/vsba/loudoun/Board.nsf/files/CD5QWY6B5CBB/$file/Clean%20LEAF%20Charter%20Final.pdf.

17. National School Boards Association, "First Amendment at Board Meetings," NSBA, October 2019, retrieved from https://www.nsba.org/ASBJ/2019/October/First-Amendment.

18. K. Lah and J. Hannah, CNN, "Students Are Fed Up with Raging Adults at School Board Meetings," KCRA.com, October 31, 2021, retrieved from https://www.kcra.com/article/students-are-fed-up-with-raging-adults-at-school-board-meetings/38115571#.

Index

About the Author

Kristen J. Amundson started her career in education policy as a kindergarten volunteer, and from there things just got out of hand. In a career that spanned more than three decades, she served as a school board member and chair, as a member of the Virginia House of Delegates, and as the CEO of the National Association of State Boards of Education.

Amundson represented the Forty-Fourth District (George Washington's old legislative district) in the Virginia General Assembly from 1999 to 2009. She was vice chair of the House Democratic Caucus and served as its political director. During her decade in the House, she also was a member of Virginia's P–16 Council and the Southern Regional Education Board.

Before her election to the General Assembly, Amundson—a former teacher—served for nearly a decade on the Fairfax County, Virginia, school board, including two years as its chair. She was the senior vice president for Education Sector, an independent think tank.

She has written extensively about education. Her book *81 Questions for Parents: Helping Your Kids Succeed in School* was published by Rowman & Littlefield in 2021. She is a frequent author of opinion pieces on education and has been published in the *Richmond Times-Dispatch* and the *Washington Post*, among others.

In 2005, with two friends, she cofounded La BECA Women's Scholarship Foundation. Since then, La BECA has provided scholarships to more than 140 women and girls in Central and South America, helping them become engineers, dentists, teachers, business leaders, and entrepreneurs. In 2020, in the midst of the COVID-19 crisis that shut schools across the United States, she cofounded EduTutorVA, a nonprofit organization that links aspiring educators with Virginia's lowest-achieving students to help close learning gaps. In 2021, she received the Distinguished Citizen Award from Macalester College, her alma mater.

Made in the USA
Las Vegas, NV
18 February 2023